DIVINE HEALING

❧ ❧ ❧ ❧ ❧ ❧

The Power of Faith

Timothy J. Dailey, Ph.D.

Timothy J. Dailey, Ph.D., earned his doctorate in theology from Marquette University and studied at Wheaton College and the Institute of Holy Land Studies, Jerusalem. He has taught theology, biblical history, and comparative religion at the Biblical Resources Study Center, Jerusalem; the Jerusalem Center for Biblical Studies; and Toccoa Falls College.

Cover photo: Shutterstock

Acknowledgments:
Page 11: Reprinted from *Priorities for Health*, Vol. 12, No. 1, 2000, published by the American Council on Science and Health
Pages 34–37, 137–138: Reprinted with the permission of Scribner, a division of Simon & Schuster, from *Timeless Healing* by Herbert Benson, M.D., with Marg Stark. Copyright © 1996 by Herbert Benson, M.D.
Pages 59–61: Courtesy of the *Fort Worth Star Telegram*
Pages 99, 103–104: Courtesy of the *Baltimore Jewish Times*
Pages 139–141: Courtesy of *The Albuquerque Tribune*
Pages 156–157: Reprinted courtesy of the *Worcester Telegram & Gazette*
Page 161: Courtesy of Barbara Kois
Pages 163–164: Henri Brickey, *The Yuma (Arizona) Daily Sun*
Page 187: Excerpt from "The Medicine of Friendship," *The Jerusalem Report*, April 24, 2000, by Judith Bolton-Fasman

ß ß ß

ISBN-13: 978-1-4508-3065-2
ISBN-10: 1-4508-3065-X

Manufactured in USA.

8 7 6 5 4 3 2 1

Table of Contents

❧ ❧ ❧

HAVE HOPE AND FAITH, AND PRAY

℘ ℘ ℘

Faith can move mountains. It can also move body and soul. That is the growing conviction of the many who have experienced faith's power in mending the body and in healing the soul.

Whether you are a skeptic or are already convinced of God's ability to heal, *Divine Healing* will help you explore the possibilities for physical, emotional, and spiritual healing in your own life. This book is filled with true stories of ordinary people whose lives God transformed because of their faith, as well as the prayers of others. But it's not just a compilation of testimonials. It also offers scientific evidence that faith, hope, and religious involvement all promote good health.

During the past two decades, dozens of controlled studies have demonstrated a positive relationship between religious faith and physical well-being. Having hope and prayer have been shown to decrease blood pressure, lower the risk of heart disease, and strengthen the immune system. The extraordinary duo, hope and faith, have also been credited with increasing the longevity of cancer patients—even those whom doctors had designated as terminal.

Divine Healing isn't just about physical health, but it's also about emotional and spiritual health. It will show you how hope and prayer can have a significant impact on your outlook and be powerful allies in the healing process. Faith can provide strength when you are weak, and it can give you a sense of purpose and serenity that is emotionally, and often physically, healing.

We'd like to believe that modern medicine can conquer all, but over time it's become apparent that medicine has limits. Doctors can't cure every disease; they can't save every person's life. Although we have lost some of our faith in the invincibility of science, we have begun to realize the importance of healing the spirit. There is an enduring link between science and spirit, a link we should try to strengthen.

There are times when both medicine and faith fail, when it seems that our prayers have not been answered. *Divine Healing* addresses those issues, too. Perhaps, at these times, healing has occurred on a deeper, more fulfilling level. The answer to our prayers could be a transformation of spirit or a healing of relationships rather than of the body. This book is about how God works miracles for us in whatever form our healing may take when we have hope, prayer, and faith.

CHAPTER 1
Healing in History

❧ ❧ ❧

In modern times, we think that doctors and religious leaders provide completely separate services. We go to the doctor for our physical problems, and we consult our clergy for matters of the soul. But this distinction is a fairly recent one. Throughout most of history, the roles of physician and clergy have been closely related. In fact, the same person often treated body and soul. Recently, Western society has started to realize what ancient people already knew: Faith, hope, worship, and spirituality can be equal partners with medicine in the fight against disease and suffering.

St. Augustine of Hippo, the great Church father, was born in A.D. 354. Although he lived many centuries ago, the prevailing beliefs about miraculous healing were similar to our own today. People then, like now, were skeptical. Augustine believed that miracles had taken place at the time of Jesus, but he thought such wonders were for a special time in history, not for his day or for future times.

Augustine's ideas about miracles changed dramatically, though, after the remains of St. Stephen, the first Christian martyr, were discovered. According to tradition, in A.D. 415, blood-red roses sprang from the ground. Underneath them were St. Stephen's bones. The bones were brought to the church in Hippo, where Augustine was bishop. They were placed in a shrine there because the early Christians believed that such relics were blessed and could bring God's favor upon individuals and churches.

This belief in the healing power of relics is based on Chapter 12 in the book of 2 Kings of the Hebrew Bible. The passage relates an incident in which a dead man was thrown into the tomb of the prophet Elisha, the disciple

and successor of the prophet Elijah, who was known as a healer. As soon as the dead man's body touched Elisha's bones, he was restored to life.

> Now bands of Moabites used to invade the land in the spring of the year. As a man was being buried, a marauding band was seen and the man was thrown into the grave of Elisha; as soon as the man touched the bones of Elisha, he came to life and stood on his feet.
>
> ❧
>
> 2 KINGS 13:20–21

It took about nine years after St. Stephen's remains were brought to Hippo, but tradition says believers in their healing power were not disappointed. Two weeks before Easter in the year 424, a brother and sister who both suffered from convulsive seizures came to North Africa to visit Hippo. They went every day to the church and prayed for healing.

On Easter Sunday the first miracle occurred. While the young man was praying at the Shrine of St. Stephen, he suddenly collapsed. At first, those in the crowd feared

that he had died. But he got up, and when he did, it was without the telltale seizures

Augustine talked with the young man and was convinced that God had indeed healed him in answer to his prayers. A couple of days later the brother and sister returned to the church for a service in which they praised God for the brother's healing. The sister still trembled uncontrollably from the seizures.

As Augustine began his sermon, the sister made her way to the shrine to pray. Soon Augustine's sermon was interrupted by a piercing scream that resounded throughout the sanctuary. The young woman, like her brother before her, had fallen to the ground unconscious. When she awakened and got up, she, too, had been completely healed.

The congregation was jubilant at this second miracle. According to Augustine, "praise to God was shouted so loud that my ears could scarcely stand the din." From that day he began to document the healings that occurred in Hippo. Some of the miracles were recorded in his great work *The City of God*. "Once I realized how many miracles were occurring in our own day... [I realized] how wrong it would be to allow the memory of these marvels of divine power to perish from among our people," Augustine wrote. "It is only two years ago that the keeping of records was begun here in Hippo, and already, at this writing, we have nearly 70 attested miracles."

Our Own Times

In the last two decades, modern medicine has begun to lose some of its skepticism about miraculous healing. Like Augustine, doctors have witnessed and patients have experienced inexplicable recoveries that appear to be the result of faith and prayer. These are being documented, much like Augustine documented the miracles at Hippo. And the healing benefits of religious belief, communal worship, and hope are now the subject of rigorous scientific exploration. Today, as we research the role that religion plays in our physical and emotional health, it is only proper that we first look back in history to see how spiritual and physical healing were once inseparable.

THE SPIRITUAL-MEDICAL PARTNERSHIP

The roles of physician and clergy have been intertwined throughout most cultures and much of history. In fact,

The deity-doctor connection has existed since antiquity. In the fifth century B.C. the Greek health practitioner Hippocrates supposedly disunited medicine and religion—and thus, popularly, has long been called the "Father of Medicine." But by no means does it seem that Hippocrates was irreligious. For example, he reportedly belonged to the sect of Aesculapius, a god of medicine and healing. Indeed, some ancient scholars noted that Hippocrates had been described as a descendent of Apollo, another medical deity, and hence as a god himself. Upon graduating medical school, many physicians in Europe and the Americas swear an oath of ethical professional behavior that is at least similar to one attributed to Hippocrates, which is a spiritual covenant.

৪

—CHARLES O. GALLINA, PH.D., *PRIORITIES*, VOLUME 12, NUMBER 1, 2000 outside of Western civilization, with its emphasis on science and technology, spirituality and medicine have long been considered equal partners in combating illness.

Ancient Egypt

The ancient Egyptians believed that each person was a product of different spiritual elements. Each person has a "ba," or soul, and a "ka," the combination of a person's physical and intellectual qualities. When these double spirits, the ka and the ba, live together in harmony, the individual lives a healthy and rewarding life.

Because they believed that both the ba and the ka need to be nurtured, Egyptian medicine used physical and nonphysical healing techniques. Prayer, medicine, and magic together played equally important roles in healing the whole person.

The Egyptians worshipped a number of gods and goddesses, many of whom, they believed, could help those who needed medical care. People called upon specific deities to prevent or cure diseases and wild animal attacks. And they directed incantations to disease-causing deities or demons, telling them to leave the body.

Some Egyptian temples were associated with healing and health care. The buildings at the temple of Hathor at Dendera, for instance, could be called infirmaries. The sick were cared for there through baths, regimens, and special diets, as well as religious prayers.

The first doctor in recorded history lived in Egypt. Imhotep, of Zoser, lived around 3000 B.C. Imhotep was so famous that he eventually gained a place in Egyptian mythology, where he was deified as the offspring of Ptah, the creator of the universe, and Sekhmet, a fierce goddess who was associated both with disease and with healing and medicine.

Imhotep was a learned man; he was an astronomer, an architect who built the first pyramid, and a physician. We know little of Imhotep's medical knowledge, but archeologists have uncovered manuscripts, written on papyrus (a paper made from reeds), that describe the use of spiritual incantations in the healing practices of ancient Egypt.

India

The healing system in ancient India was called *Ayurveda*, a word meaning "life knowledge." Indian medicine used both herbs and other natural substances as well as magic. It was the job of the *bhishaj*, or medical practitioner, to rid his patients of disease. He used a variety of means,

from exorcising the disease demons from inside the body to mending a broken bone.

Ayurveda is a religious concept that emphasizes the connection between all living things and the Creator. According to this belief, the body is composed of five basic elements: ether, air, fire, water, and earth. When these elements are out of balance, the result is sickness and disease. Priests used the Atharva Veda, an ancient Indian religious text dealing with the medical sciences, as their main source of information about treatment.

Native America

Ancient Native North Americans believed in the Great Spirit that inhabited all living things and kept nature and humanity in perfect balance. Religion and the healing arts were not practiced separately from one another. The medicine man, the priest, and the healer all used incantations as well as natural remedies to help people get well.

Although there are similarities among them, different Native American peoples used different approaches to the treatment of physical and spiritual illness. Shamanism (perhaps the first kind of medicine ever practiced, a form of spirituality in which everything, even inanimate objects, has a soul), herbal remedies, healing ceremonies, and other forms of spiritual healing, however, are common to most Native American cultures.

The belief that being in rhythm with nature would make the body healthier was also common to most Native Americans. So, too, was the understanding that belief plays an important role in physical wellness.

The Jewish People

The Jewish rabbinic tradition did not include the use of magic and incantations. Sorcery was believed to be of the devil, and Hebrew religious texts were not allowed to be used in any way that would mimic such practices. In his Code, the 12th century Jewish philosopher/physician Maimonides cautions: "If you whisper a spell over a wound while reciting a verse from the Torah or recite a verse over a child to save it from terrors, or place a scroll or phylacteries on an infant to induce it to sleep, you are not only included in the category of sorcerers and soothsayers but among those who repudiate the Torah. For these people use the words of the Torah as

a cure of the body whereas they are exclusively a cure of the soul" (*Hilchot Avodah Zarah* 11:12). Similarly, the *Talmud Shavuoth 15b* prohibits healing the body using sacred words or objects.

The ancient Israelites were commanded to seek healing from the Lord. In fact, the Hebrew Bible contains only one reference to doctors: "Is there no balm in Gilead? Is there no physician there? Why then has the health of my poor people not been restored?" (Jeremiah 8:22). Instead, for various maladies the Israelites were commanded to go to the priest: "The Lord spoke to Moses and Aaron, saying: When a person has on the skin of his body a swelling or an eruption or a spot, and it turns into a leprous disease on the skin of his body, then he shall be brought to Aaron the priest or to one of his sons the priests" (Leviticus 13:1–2).

The ancient Jewish "Misheberakh" prayer, which is still recited during the Torah service today, reflects this call upon God for healing. During the prayer of blessing the rabbi requests healing for those who are infirm. At that point in the service, members of the congregation may approach the *bimah* (where the Torah is read) and ask for healing on behalf of a sick relative or friend.

HEALING IN THE FIRST CENTURY

The first century was an age of the expectant belief in miracles. This widespread belief in miraculous healing at the time of Jesus is confirmed by evidence uncovered by archeologists.

The popular cult of Aesculapius, for instance, was a reaction against the Greco-Roman attitude toward sickness. The Greeks and Romans considered illness and disease a matter of fate, and they believed that, compared to the soul, the physical body had little intrinsic

Hoping for a Cure
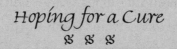

New light was shed on the story of Jesus at the Pool of Bethesda, related in the Gospel of John, in 1950, when archeologists uncovered a pagan sanctuary to Aesculapius adjoining the pool. This temple was likely the reason why the Gospel records that "many invalids—blind, lame, and paralyzed" were found in the vicinity of the pool. They were hoping for a cure.

value. When someone became ill, it was assumed that the gods were displeased with them. The Aesculapius cult offered hope to those living in a society that was indifferent to human suffering and that could do little to alleviate many illnesses.

More than 200 shrines devoted to the healing god Aesculapius have been found throughout ancient Greece and Rome. The sick and infirm would make a pilgrimage to these shrines to offer a sacrifice, then they would immerse themselves in a ritual pool in hopes of a cure.

In contrast to Greco-Roman philosophy, the Jewish doctrine taught that humans are a unity of body and soul: The body has real value and is worthy of respect. That is why the Hebrews preserved the body by reverently placing it in tombs, unlike the Greeks and Romans, who commonly cremated or otherwise destroyed bodily remains.

The significance and value of the body is affirmed throughout the New Testament. The Apostle Paul writes: "Do you not know that you are God's temple and that God's Spirit dwells in you? If anyone destroys God's temple, God will destroy that person. For God's temple is holy, and you are that temple" (1 Corinthians 3:16–17).

The concept of the resurrection of the dead at the end of time is unique to Judaism, Christianity, and Islam. It teaches us that our bodies are not disposable but that they should be considered as a sacred trust. Therefore, we should make every effort to maintain and heal our bodies.

This belief is not mere philosophical speculation. Through the centuries it has been translated into concrete action. The conviction that our bodies are valuable and important continues to serve as a motivation for many churches and religious ministries. Kate Lindberg, pastor, coordinator of pastoral care, at First Presbyterian Church of Wheaton, Illinois, says: "Our healing ministry grows out of our understanding that God came in the flesh, and our bodies need to be honored and cared for. It embodies our concern for people's health as we pray for healing and renewal of the whole person."

Similarly, the prayer of the Holy Communion service of the Anglican Church, spoken as the bread and wine are administered to the congregation, reflects the hope for restoration of the body as well as the soul: "May the body of our Lord, Jesus Christ . . . preserve thy body and soul unto everlasting life."

HEALING IN THE CHURCH

The early Church father Justin Martyr lived in the beginning of the second century after Christ. He was an educated man who taught philosophy in Rome, the most cosmopolitan city of the time. In his *Apology*, Justin Martyr writes about numerous healings that occurred, including the raising of the dead. The Christians had such undeniable power over disease that the emperor, in his ignorance, could only attribute it to demonic powers.

Again and again during the first few centuries of the Christian era we find testimonies about physical healing in the writings of the Church fathers. However, the attitude of the Church started to change, beginning with Pope Gregory the Great, bishop of Rome between A.D. 590 and 604.

Gregory ruled over the Church at a time of exceptional social crisis. Barbarians had already sacked the once invincible Rome, and on every front the empire was reeling from attack. People began to feel that God was punishing the Christianized Roman Empire and that illness was one means of divine punishment.

By the Middle Ages much of Western Christianity believed that sickness was the punishment for sinful behavior. People suffering from illness were instructed to

Preaching and Healing
❦ ❦ ❦

Once there was a man covered with leprosy. When he saw Jesus, he bowed with his face to the ground and begged him to make him clean.

Then Jesus stretched out his hand, touched him, and said, "I do choose. Be made clean." Immediately the leprosy left him.

Jesus ordered him to tell no one. "Go," he said, "and show yourself to the priest, and, as Moses commanded, make an offering for your cleansing, for a testimony to them."

But now the word about Jesus spread abroad; many crowds would gather to hear him and to be cured of their diseases (Luke 5:12–15).

Jesus also sent out his disciples to heal people. "As you go, proclaim the good news, 'The kingdom of heaven has come near.' Cure the sick, raise the dead, cleanse the lepers, cast out demons. You received without payment; give without payment" (Matthew 10:7–8). The disciples did as they were commanded.

summon a priest before a doctor so that the cause of the illness—sinfulness—could be expunged, allowing the person to become healthy again. In the 14th century, Europe was ravaged by the Black Death, which killed tens of millions of people. A Papal Bull issued in 1348 spoke of the "pestilence with which God is afflicting the Christian people."

While Western Christians believed that sickness was a divine judgment, evidence indicates that their pastors practiced the healing arts. When America was a British colony, for instance, its clergymen were also its doctors. In those days preachers were expected to be healers.

SECULARISM REPLACES SPIRITUALITY

The partnership between faith and medicine began to unravel in the 17th century as a result of the scientific revolution. Science began to create its own miracles—without reference to any higher power. By the 20th century, there were antiseptics to prevent infections during childbirth and surgery, as well as antibiotics to cure dangerous infections. Diseases that once crippled and killed millions could now be prevented by immunization.

As time passed, scientists learned more about the mysterious workings of the human body. They learned how blood circulates through the body, and they discovered the existence of bacteria and viruses—and even the building block of the human genome—DNA, or deoxyribonucleic acid.

As scientists learned more about the physical causes and cures of illness, they increasingly downplayed the ancient knowledge that the mind, spirit, and environment all have important roles in the body's health. Drugs and technology held sway over the medical establishment, while belief in divine intervention through prayer soon fell by the wayside, dismissed as a throwback to a more superstitious age.

MODERN MEDICINE COMES FULL CIRCLE

Until the scientific revolution, the healing arts combined medicine with faith. Now it seemed that faith was no longer necessary. The Irish-born playwright George Bernard Shaw, born in 1856, observed, "We have not lost faith, but we have transferred it from God to the medical profession." It was widely assumed that there were no limits to what modern medicine could accomplish. It was just a matter of time before a cure was found for every remaining disease. And if modern science could explain what was once unexplainable— and cure what was once incurable—who needed God?

Over time, however, it became apparent that modern medicine has limitations. Some ailments refuse to be conquered. Society continues to be afflicted with debilitating and deadly viruses, despite the concerted efforts of modern medicine. And in recent years, scientists have discovered that some of the most dangerous killers in Western culture—heart disease and cancer—are often caused by preventable factors such as smoking, obesity, and lack of exercise.

Health care practitioners are beginning to realize that medication and surgery are not the only tools available to make people well. Insight into the emotional or mental underpinnings of disease is also necessary. Healing of the spirit is vital component in physical healing. The link between spirit, mind, and body is powerful—one that is not easily broken or ignored.

CHAPTER 2
Worship and Wellness

❧ ❧ ❧

Polls not only show that nearly all Americans believe in God—but that we are also a nation of pray-ers. Seventy-five percent of us believe that prayer can speed recovery, and one in every seven people believe that they themselves have been healed. Is it just wishful thinking—the "placebo effect"? Not so, according to Herbert Benson, M.D., associate professor of medicine at Harvard Medical School. Benson argues that faith in God carries even more power than faith in medical treatment or in one's physician.

It only takes a few minutes for our complacent lives to be changed forever. It happened to Gary and Tina Manweiler in their doctor's office. Gary had gone to the doctor to ask about what he assumed was merely a troublesome abscess in his mouth. The sober look on the doctor's face as he examined Gary told him something was wrong.

The doctor didn't mince words: The "abscess" was likely a cancerous tumor. He performed a biopsy and sent the Manweilers home in shock. Gary appeared calm, but Tina's tears began before the doctor's office door closed behind them.

The tears didn't stop for two days. Finally, Tina pulled out a pen and paper and started pouring out her fears and confusion in a letter to God. "Dear God," wrote Tina, "You know how much I love Gary. Do your will for him and for us. Give us strength to handle whatever situation arises." As the words quickly flowed onto the paper, they were smudged by her tears.

Tina returned to her job at the post office with a heavy heart, but with a calming sense of having shared her burden with perhaps the only one who could help.

On the way home from work, she happened to turn on a gospel station. She hadn't listened to this kind of music for a long time, and she found the beautiful songs quieting to her spirit. The announcer came on and seemed to speak directly to Tina. She said someone was listening to us who hears our every need and who would answer our every prayer—someone who loves and watches over us all the time.

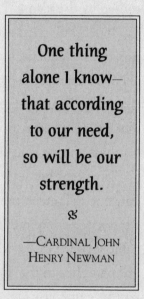

One thing alone I know— that according to our need, so will be our strength.

§

—CARDINAL JOHN HENRY NEWMAN

Tina's letter had been answered.

She knew God was watching over her and had heard her prayer. He knew what she needed and how much she could handle. From that moment Tina's tears dried up, and she exuded new confidence.

When the call came to meet with the doctor, Tina feared what the test results would show. Still, an overwhelming, unexplainable peace filled her spirit. As they entered the doctor's office, Tina carried the letter in her pocket. Gary was told he had cancer but that it was treatable. He was told that since the tumor was pressing

against his eye, the surgery to remove it would likely result in the loss of his eye.

The following week Gary underwent an 11-hour surgery coupled with plastic surgery to repair the damage caused by the tumor. His eye was also removed.

"Success!" cried the surgeon afterward. Gary's prognosis was excellent, but he still had a long, hard road ahead of him. He began a series of radiation treatments that caused painful blisters in his mouth. In only four months, Gary went from 209 pounds to 137 pounds and lost hair on one side of his head.

Tina kept her letter to God close to her during Gary's battle with cancer, never losing hope that he would experience complete healing. Strangers and friends also came forward in the Manweilers' hour of need. Different churches in the area offered prayer and support, and pastors came visiting. "Jesus and his angels—even secret ones—really took good care of us," says Tina. "And they still do."

More than a year later, the doctors are optimistic, and the Manweilers' life is beginning to return to normal. Still, Tina keeps her letter and its message of hope close to her heart. The help that Tina received from above made the critical difference in her ability to cope during

Gary's bout with life-threatening cancer. She now knows that prayer is a resource to call upon in tough times, like drawing water from a well when you are thirsty.

"But there's no need to wait until trouble strikes to call upon God's strength and guidance for daily life," cautions Tina, "It's so easy to worry about silly, small things, but faith keeps you clear about what matters."

AMERICANS HAVE FAITH

Polls show that 95 percent of Americans believe in God. But they aren't just believers; they are also pray-ers. A survey by the Barna Research Group found that nearly 90 percent of Americans say they pray to God, and 60 percent pray more than once a day. A Gallup Poll reports that 42 percent of Americans attend religious services regularly, and nearly three-quarters of the poll respondents agreed with the statement, "My whole approach to life is based on my religion."

Can an individual's attitude and religious beliefs have an impact on the healing process? A USA WEEKEND poll found that 79 percent of Americans believe that faith does play a role in helping people recover from illness or injury. Many of these people ground their belief in personal experiences. Incredibly, 56 percent said they have experienced the healing power of religious faith in their own lives. A CNN/Time poll found that more than 75 percent of Americans believe that God sometimes heals people who are seriously ill, and 73 percent believe that praying for others can help speed their recovery.

A study measuring the helpfulness of prayer found that 96 percent of patients facing heart surgery prayed. Another study similarly reported that 73 percent of hospitalized patients prayed.

Yet another survey found that one of every seven people polled believed God had healed them. The miraculous cures occurred for all types of illnesses—everything from simple viruses to back pain to cancer.

So, not only do most Americans believe in God, they believe in a healing God. And research provides ample evidence that Americans want their doctors to acknowledge this belief. The USA WEEKEND poll found that 63 percent of Americans think it's a good idea for doctors to talk with patients about the role faith plays in healing. And, according to the CNN/Time poll, 64 percent said doctors

> **Not only do most Americans believe in God, they believe in a healing God.**

should pray with their patients when the patients ask them to. In one Gallup Poll, 77 percent of respondents said doctors should consider the spiritual needs of their patients, and 48 percent wanted their doctors to pray with them.

MORE THAN THE PLACEBO EFFECT

Like so many, Colleen and Alan Armstrong did not have a doctor who prayed for them when Alan became sick. Nevertheless, they were blessed with a strong sense of not being alone.

When Alan began experiencing lower back pain, his doctor attributed it to muscle strain. After all, he was extremely busy. He was taking night classes in addition to working, and he had a wife and two active teenagers. Alan learned to live with the back pain, but a few months later he began to feel extremely fatigued. More ominously, he started losing weight. Finally, he saw a specialist, who immediately ordered a CAT scan.

The results were shattering. Alan had a very large malignant tumor on his kidney. It had grown out of the kidney and up the main artery toward the heart. The tumor was in a very advanced stage and required immediate surgery.

The Armstrongs entered the darkest period of their lives. The risks in the surgery were very high, and the prognosis was not good. Everything they believed in would be put to the test. Colleen spent sleepless nights crying out to God, begging to feel his presence as she contemplated a future without the person most dear to her. Daily she claimed every promise from God's Word that she had ever been taught.

One evening before the surgery, Colleen helped her weakened husband into bed for the night. She covered him, prayed with him, and turned out the light. As she was leaving the room, she was flooded with sadness and pity for her husband, lying there alone in the dark. She called out, "Alan, are you afraid to be left alone in there?"

Alan's simple reply would carry her through the difficult days ahead. "Colleen, I'm not alone in here," he replied.

It was then that she knew that the scriptural promise that God would provide a peace that surpasses all understanding was very real. With two major surgeries behind them and months of chemotherapy, scans, and uncertainty ahead, the Armstrongs are living testimonies to God's faithfulness and provision. Although rough times come and go, and tears still flow, they hold firm to the promise given in Philippians 4:7, the promise that God continues to fulfill: "the peace of God, which surpasses all understanding, will guard [your] hearts and your minds in Christ Jesus."

IS FAITH A PLACEBO?

Despite the Armstrongs' moving testimony, some would argue that their faith was just wishful thinking. After all, almost anything a person believes in can, in one way or another, have a positive impact. The power of this "placebo effect" has been illustrated again and again. In the past, for example, there was a variety of treatments for angina pectoris, which is pain in the chest and arms. (One of the more exotic treatments involved injections of cobra venom.) For a time, doctors expected such treatments to work, so they assured patients that their conditions would be cured. Up to 90 percent of the time they were right. But later, as the cause of angina pectoris was better understood, doctors soon doubted the reliability of such treatments. The rate of effectiveness dropped as low as 30 percent.

Is it possible, then, that the healing power of faith is nothing more than the placebo effect?

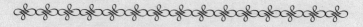

In *Timeless Healing*, Herbert Benson, M.D., associate professor of medicine at Harvard Medical School, writes, "Faith in the medical treatment, faith in the health care provider, and faith in the relationship forged between you and your healer are wonderfully therapeutic, successful in treating 60 percent to 90 percent of the most common medical problems. But if you so believe, faith in an invincible and infallible force carries even more healing power."

In another book, *The Relaxation Response*, Benson explains a simple technique that he discovered could, among other effects, lower a person's blood pressure and muscle tension. The technique, called the relaxation response, requires repeating a word or phrase (or a sound or a muscle activity) for several minutes. Any thoughts that interrupt the repetition are passively ignored. If individuals practice repeating a word or phrase while ignoring all other thoughts, they will experience the physiologic effects of slowed heart rate, slowed breathing, decreased blood pressure, and muscle relaxation.

Benson knew the power of the placebo effect. He was not surprised to find that patients who believed most in the technique experienced the greatest benefits from it. But Benson also observed something that he couldn't

The Ancient Power of Placebo
♂ ♂ ♂

The "placebo effect" is a well-known modern concept. But, although the terminology is rather contemporary, the practice itself is not. "Primitive physicians showed their wisdom by treating the whole person—soul as well as body. At times, treatments and medicines that produced no physical effects, nevertheless, could make a patient feel better," writes Carol Lewis in "Medical Milestones of the Last Millennium" (*FDA Consumer* magazine, March-April 2000). "Ironically, this so-called 'placebo effect' remains applicable even in clinical medicine today."

have predicted. About 80 percent of his patients, when instructed to choose a pleasant word or phrase to repeat, chose a religious word or a prayer. And those patients benefitted even more from the technique than those who simply believed in the technique itself.

Benson writes, "I already knew that eliciting the relaxation response could 'disconnect' everyday thoughts

and worries, calming people's bodies and minds more quickly and to a degree otherwise unachievable. It appeared that beliefs added to the response transported the mind/body even more dramatically, quieting worries and fears significantly better than the relaxation response alone. And I speculated that religious faith was more influential than other affirmative beliefs.

"Our studies demonstrated that people feel an increase in spirituality relatively quickly upon eliciting the relaxation response but that the longer one makes the elicitation part of one's routine, the more these sensations grow. Like the physical rewards we had measured, spirituality also seemed to be cumulative, increasing over time as people regularly elicited the response.

"But what exactly were people experiencing that felt spiritual to them? When we compiled the results, some common themes emerged. People who reported increased spirituality after eliciting the relaxation response described two things about the experience: 1) the presence of an energy, a force, a power—God— that was beyond themselves, and 2) this presence felt close to them."

Further research proved Benson to be correct. Those who "felt this presence" noted the greatest medical benefits. "Faith in God . . . seems to be particularly influential in healing because 'God,' by all definitions of which I am aware, is boundless and limitless," Benson concludes.

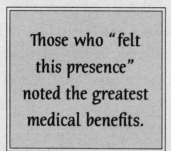

Those who "felt this presence" noted the greatest medical benefits.

"It is part of our nature to believe in an almighty power lest our health be undermined by the ultimate and dreadful fact—that we may succumb to illness and that all of us must die."

Stephen G. Post, Ph.D., associate director of the Center for Biomedical Ethics at Case Western Reserve University, agrees. In an article in *Mind/Body Medicine*, he wrote, "As innumerable theologians have indicated, persons wish to protect themselves through the security of daily routines that provide order and control over existence. When illness breaks in—especially severe and disruptive illness—the routine is quickly pushed aside by in-breaking waves of chaos. It is like awakening in the morning to find a flood at the back door that disrupts the veneer of daily order and regularity. During illness, people realize that the routine is ultimately not real because human beings are fragile and subject to contingencies over which they hold no ultimate control. At this point,

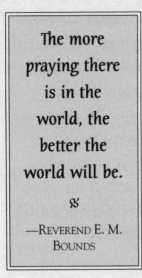

> The more praying there is in the world, the better the world will be.
>
> ❧
>
> —REVEREND E. M. BOUNDS

many patients call out to some higher being in the universe, who, in contrast to ourselves, does have things under control. One need not be a believer to recognize the existential value of religion in coping with the illness experience...."

One significant result of all this research is a better reputation for "faith healing." Of course, there will always be individuals who play on the fears of sick people and promise miraculous cures—for financial or personal gain. But this unfortunate fact should not detract from evidence that faith can heal—sometimes miraculously.

We've heard of such cases—and perhaps even experienced it ourselves: A person with a fatal disease declares that God is going to heal him, and his illness disappears. We pray for someone who is sick and the person gets well. A growing number of what the medical profession calls spontaneous remissions—and the rest of us call miracles—have been documented. One list of medically unexplained healings includes 3,000 cases.

THE POWER OF PRAYER

Witek Krajewski was in the peak of health. At 44 he was active in sports. His weekly schedule included coaching judo (he'd earned his black belt in Poland as a teenager), playing soccer (outdoors, all year—in Iowa!), basketball, and jogging.

Witek was probably involved in too many sports, but he told himself he needed that to relieve the pressures of a demanding job. He was proud of his low blood pressure and slow heart rate. At his last physical exam, several doctors had admired the results of his stress EKG.

One morning in March 1998, Witek woke up with a sharp pain in his back. He could hardly get up, and breathing was painful. Thinking he had pulled a muscle playing basketball the day before, Witek put on a cold pack and took some pain relievers before leaving for work.

That afternoon he called his wife, Sonja. From his labored breathing she knew immediately something was wrong. She took Witek to the doctor, who after a quick exam diagnosed a pulled muscle. After learning that Witek spent several hours sitting at the computer the night before, the doctor suggested that this was the cause of his strained muscle.

Witek and Sonja glanced at each other. He was used to spending time at the computer—there had to be another cause for his backache. Sonja asked the doctor about Witek's painful breathing: Was he going to listen to his lungs? The doctor didn't seem to think it was necessary. Frankly, he had sicker patients to attend to than a strapping fellow who, other than a pulled muscle, was in the peak of health. He prescribed a muscle relaxant and sent Witek and Sonja home with assurances that Witek would soon be back on the soccer field.

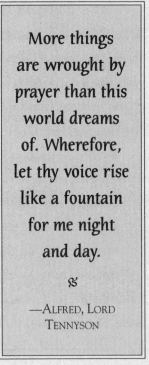

More things are wrought by prayer than this world dreams of. Wherefore, let thy voice rise like a fountain for me night and day.

&

—ALFRED, LORD TENNYSON

But things didn't get better. Within hours, Witek's temperature rose alarmingly. He began to shake, his pain grew worse, and he seemed disoriented. Sonja reached the emergency room doctor, who had her increase the pain medication, thinking Witek probably had picked up a virus in addition to the pulled muscle.

Over the next day and a half, Witek didn't improve. A different muscle relaxant was prescribed, but by then he could barely sit up to watch TV. The news was on, and Sonja heard a report about an outbreak of a deadly strain of strep in Texas and in Illinois. That couldn't be it—after all, they lived in Iowa. Still, the report was worrisome enough that Sonja took her weakened husband to the emergency room.

The doctors realized that Witek was desperately ill. Blood tests indicated an infection, but it could be days before the specific bacteria could be identified. Witek was put on antibiotics in the hospital but continued to deteriorate.

The next day the grim diagnosis came back: invasive Strep A. Witek also had rapidly increasing congestion in his lungs and damage to his heart.

Invasive Strep A is related to the infamous flesh-eating bacteria, but it destroys from the inside out. It causes a blood-borne infection a thousand times deadlier than ordinary strep and attacks the patient's internal organs, especially the heart. The doctors told Sonja that Witek should be transferred immediately to the nearby University of Iowa Hospitals and Clinics, one of the Midwest's top medical centers.

Scores of doctors and interns visited Witek's small cubicle in the intensive care unit, where he was connected to a variety of monitors. The senior physician took Sonja aside. "I'm sure you realize how serious the situation is," he said. "At this point your husband's chances are 50/50. How he does tonight will tell us whether he will survive."

Sonja couldn't believe what the doctor was saying. "Oh yes," he said, emphatically, "This disease is a killer. It's very, very virulent."

In shock and filled with dread, Sonja had to return home to see about their children. She found a message on her answering machine from her friend Sheila.

"Don't worry. We're praying for him," Sheila said. She told Sonja that she had given Witek's name to a prayer group that held 24-hour prayer vigils. They agreed to pray for Witek for 30 days.

Like many people, Sonja didn't often take time for prayer in the hustle and bustle of daily life. But now, with her husband's life literally hanging in the balance, with no "magic bullet" miracle drugs to ensure recovery, she realized that there was no one left to turn to but God.

Sonja's mother called from 2,000 miles away and offered to telephone family and friends. "If people want to know what they can do to help, I'll ask them to pray," she said. Sonja was grateful to the prayer warriors who were interceding for her husband. She found herself joining with them fervently.

The spirit was willing, but the flesh was weak, and Sonja soon collapsed exhausted into bed. When she called the next morning, the nurse said Witek had not gotten any worse. Sonja's heart leaped at the wonderful news!

> "If people want to know what they can do to help, I'll ask them to pray," she said.

Witek began to improve. The doctors, however, cautioned that he had suffered some damage to his heart, although they didn't know how much. In any case, his recovery would take a long time.

That night when Sonja went home, she found more than 15 messages from friends and family with offers of help ranging from prayer to childcare. When she fell into bed, it was with deep gratitude to God and to the network of friends, family, and others—some of whom she and Witek didn't even know—who were sending prayers and help.

Over the next few days the doctors conducted tests to determine how much damage Witek's heart had sustained. Miraculously, the valve that had been "full of vegetation" in the earlier X ray was now clear. Witek had escaped permanent damage to his heart and other organs.

Witek could barely stand for his first walk a few days later, needing both Sonja and a railing for support. But he persisted with each painful step, and with the help of Sonja and other family and friends, he gradually increased his duration and distance.

After a month Witek began to slowly jog. He told his wife that it had been a lifelong dream to run a marathon and that he was determined to do it. He developed a training schedule and stuck to it throughout the summer.

Finally his dream came true. Witek found himself standing among thousands of runners amassed in Chicago on a chilly morning in October. Twenty-six long, hard miles of pavement lay ahead of him, but long after most of the other runners and the crowd had gone home, an exhausted but elated Witek crossed the finish line.

"During the run," he said, "I had time to think. And I realized that it was not important how fast I could do it, just that I could do it. I was thankful just to be alive, to be there, to be able to run at all."

The marathon was the culmination of a long and difficult journey for Witek. But with the powerful combination of prayer and perseverance, he had triumphed over adversity.

PRAYER—CHAMPION OF HEALTH

Witek's doctor told him he had a killer virus. Yet he experienced a remarkable recovery, one that he and his wife attribute to the power of prayer, which was greater than the pathogen that afflicted Witek's body.

Today researchers are interested in discovering the role of prayer in health and healing. The first important scientific study of healing prayer, the Byrd Study (named after its lead researcher, Randolph Byrd), was published in 1988. The study evaluated the effect of prayer over a period of ten months on 393 patients with heart disease who were admitted to the coronary care unit at San Francisco General Hospital.

The patients were divided into two groups: one that was prayed for and one that wasn't. The patients knew that they were part of a study on prayer, but neither they

> By an impressive margin, patients who were prayed for did better than patients in the control group.

nor the medical personnel knew which group they were in. As far as Byrd knew, no one was praying for the patients in the control group; he had arranged to have the patients in the other group prayed for.

The results: By an impressive margin, patients who were prayed for did better than patients in the control group. The group of patients receiving prayer had only 27 total complications, compared with 44 complications in the control group. They had 3 cases of pneumonia compared with 13 cases in the control group, 8 cases of congestive heart failure compared with 20 cases in the control group, and 3 cases of cardiac arrest compared with 14 cases in the control group.

Prayed-for patients also were less likely to need antibiotics and diuretics. And none of the patients in the prayed-for group had to be intubated, while 12 patients in the control group required this medical procedure. (Intubation is the insertion of a tube to maintain the patient's airway.)

More Research

The Saudia Study, the next major study, looked at the effects of prayer when patients prayed for themselves. Reported in 1991, this study investigated how prayer could affect patients' feelings rather than their physical symptoms. Of 100 patients who were scheduled for coronary artery bypass surgery, 96 prayed for themselves. Two other patients who did not pray had other individuals pray for them; the remaining two patients did not use prayer at all. At the end of the study, 97 of the 100 patients said that prayer had been very helpful to them in coping with the stress of serious illness.

One of the most unusual—some say corny—studies of the power of prayer didn't focus on health, or even on people. Karl Goodfellow, a Methodist minister in Iowa who was working on his seminary doctoral project, ran across some research that showed that corn seeds that were prayed for grew better than corn seeds that received no spiritual assistance. (Although it may seem unusual to some, prayer experiments have been done on all kinds of plants and animals. Like the human studies, those studies generally indicate that all living things respond positively to prayer.)

> **The Lord keeps watch over you as you come and go, both now and forever.**
>
> ❦
>
> —PSALM 121, NIV

The people in Goodfellow's area—most of whom were farmers—began to pray for their corn. Yields increased.

Goodfellow then reached the conclusion that if God cared about corn, he must also care about the people who were growing it. But some of the locals were losing their farms. Others had suffered physical injuries from pushing themselves to exhaustion. So Goodfellow lined up "prayer partners" for every one of the 12,000 farm families in his district. Each prayer partner prayed for 10 farm families, by name, and prayed specifically for increased harvests and safety for those workers.

Larry Dossey, M.D., who summarizes Goodfellow's story in his book *Prayer Is Good Medicine*, reports, "Since the prayer project began, farmers have begun to report interesting experiences—'things that have happened that could have been disasters but weren't.' One farmer was sucked into a gravity wagon of grain, which could have suffocated him, but he was pulled out unharmed.

Another farmer near Hawkeye was driving a combine down the road when a semi trailer pulled in front of him. Only a 'miracle' prevented what should have been a fatal collision."

While Goodfellow's experiment started as more of a spiritual project than a scientific one, the University of Iowa decided to assist him in his investigation. Meanwhile, Goodfellow has been working to get prayer support for all of Iowa's 100,000 farmers.

Demonstrating that prayer is actually responsible for improved physical and emotional health can be an elusive goal. This is because it is difficult to maintain controlled studies when investigating the role of faith in healing. For example, in the Byrd Study, researchers had no way of knowing if people in the control group—those who were not being prayed for—actually had family members or friends praying for them.

PRAYER—A VALID PRESCRIPTION?

According to the scientific method, a study must yield results that are repeatable in order to be considered valid. But prayer doesn't work that way. It is not 100 percent effective. In other words, we don't always get what we pray for.

If prayer doesn't work uniformly, should it be used at all? If someone—a clergyperson, relative, or physician—encourages a person with a serious disease to pray for healing, is that person guilty of encouraging the patient with false hope?

Fortunately the cumulative result of numerous studies gives us confidence that prayer works. Dossey writes, "More than 130 controlled laboratory studies show, in general, that prayer or a prayerlike state of compassion, empathy, and love can bring about healthful changes in many types of living things, from humans to bacteria... This does not mean prayer always works, any more than drugs and surgery always work, but that, statistically speaking, prayer is effective."

From this point of view, the question is not, "Is it unethical to prescribe prayer?" but, "Is it unethical to fail to prescribe a treatment that has been shown, in many cases, to be effective?" Dossey, for one, decided that not praying for his patients "was the equivalent of withholding a needed medication or surgical procedure, and I began to pray for my patients daily."

The many ways of praying pose a host of questions for researchers. Is nonverbal prayer more effective than verbal prayer? Is prayer only effective when many people pray, or are one individual's prayers enough to evoke a response? Only future investigations of prayer and healing can answer these questions.

THE POSITIVE EFFECT OF FAITH

How does faith make people healthier? Even when there is little or no improvement in a person's physical condition, faith can make a significant difference in one's emotional outlook. Religious patients studied by Harold G. Koenig, M.D., an associate professor of psychiatry, associate professor of medicine, and director of the Center for the Study of Religion/Spirituality and Health at Duke University Medical Center, reported five ways that their faith helped them cope with serious illness.

⚘ First, these patients said their faith gave them hope for healing. Barring that, faith ultimately gave them hope for life after death. Unlike those who faced the unknown with dread and fear, patients with strong faith were able to face the future with composure and serenity.

⚘ Second, the patients said their faith gave them a sense of control. Even when the doctors had given up, they believed that an all-powerful God was able and willing to respond to their prayers. "Patients say they talk

> The act of praying, in the context of illness, is the act of taking control of a situation that seems out of control. When we pray, we do something, despite the fact that there may be nothing to do. When we take that action, when we pray, we show that illness has not rendered us powerless because illness has not silenced us.
>
> ℘
>
> —RABBI ELANA KANTER, OF BIRMINGHAM, ALABAMA, WRITING IN THE MAY 15, 1998 ISSUE OF *SH'MA, A JOURNAL OF JEWISH RESPONSIBILITY*

to God," Koenig reports in *Mind/Body Medicine*, "turn over their problems into His hands, and trust Him to orchestrate the best possible outcome. They can then stop worrying about their problems, and consequently experience comfort and peace."

↝ Third, the patients said their faith gave them strength to face their illness. While those who had no religious faith floundered in a sea of fear and panic, with no one to turn to for help, those who sought help from above experienced the promise found in the Book of Philippians: "Do not worry about anything, but in everything by prayer and supplication with thanksgiving let your requests be made known to God. And the peace of God, which surpasses all understanding, will guard your hearts and your minds in Christ Jesus" (4:6).

❧ Fourth, the patients said their faith gave them meaning—a way to make sense of their illness and pain. One of the first questions we all ask ourselves when we become seriously ill or injured is, "Why?" If a patient believes that his or her illness is a punishment from God, the effect can be harmful, causing guilt and increased suffering. But a patient who believes that God allows suffering into people's lives to build their character and help them avoid greater pain in the future can actually find a positive message in pain.

❧ Finally, the patients said their faith gave them a sense of purpose. Koenig gives the example of an elderly woman who was completely paralyzed by a stroke. She could only move her eyelids. The woman's pastor asked her to pray for various people in her church, which she did. Not only did the woman have the satisfaction of being useful, she also was visited by people in the church who told her all the ways in which her prayers were being answered. "The point of this case," Koenig writes, "is that religious people, no matter how disabled, still possess some gift or talent that they can use to serve their God."

HOW FAITH GIVES US STRENGTH

Hope, control, strength, meaning, and purpose all make us feel better. We have all experienced their positive effects. But how can these feelings actually make our bodies healthier? How can feelings of hope and strength cause broken bones to mend, cancer cells to disappear, and painful surgical wounds to quickly heal?

Memories, of course, trigger feelings. But science is now discovering that memories are not just emotional events, but physical events as well. In fact, it seems that the emotions that memories inspire are actually a result of physical changes that take place in the brain.

When you remember a certain event—think of the happiest moment in your life—you can experience the same emotions you felt at that moment, albeit to a lesser degree. Why? Research shows that the same pattern of activity occurs in your brain that occurred there during the first event.

In a very real, physical way, your brain reconstructs the event, both emotionally and physically. When you remember a happy event, you will likely smile. Recalling a loss will once again make your heart sorrowful. And when you think of a frightening event, your heartbeat may quicken, even though you know you are not in any danger.

> **Belief in God seems to trigger patterns of brain activity that have intense healing effects on the body.**

Imagine the power your brain would have if it were fueled with feelings of hope, strength, and joy! Could those feelings trigger activity in the brain that would send signals throughout the body to mend and to heal? If so, this could explain why positive thinking helps to heal.

But positive thinking alone usually isn't enough. It takes something—*someone*—who is able to help. That's why religious belief in a higher power that is absolutely strong, wise, and loving is the most powerful healer. It should call forth an unassailable force of hope and strength. And it does! Belief in God seems to trigger patterns of brain activity that have intense healing effects on the body.

Prayer Without Words

❦ ❦ ❦

Prayer is common to all the world's religions. But prayer doesn't require words. Sometimes we ask for divine assistance through actions, as in the laying on of hands.

A study in the Netherlands tested the effects of the laying on of hands on three groups of patients with high blood pressure. Once a week for 15 weeks, one group received the laying on of hands administered by people trained in the technique. The second group received "healing thoughts" from people in another room. The third group was the control group and received neither treatment.

Interestingly, the blood pressure of patients in all three groups decreased. The various treatments seemed to have no significant effect on physical health. But the patients who received the laying on of hands reported a much greater sense of well-being than patients in the other two groups.

If this process really works, anyone should be able to unleash powerful healing effects when inspired by religion. Such thoughts should trigger brain activity that produces both positive feelings and physical healing.

There are specific faith activities that seem to have the most powerful healing effects. For example, participation in religious activities is very helpful, because such rituals reinforce strong, positive memories of encounters with God. As we shall see, the ritual of prayer has also been shown to be powerfully healing.

Researchers are convinced that certain memories, thoughts, and feelings trigger similar brain activity in all human beings. For example, studies have found that a fear of snakes is virtually universal, although it is stronger in some people than in others. (Most people, in the presence of a snake, experience the familiar physical manifestations of fear: increased heart and breathing rates, trembling, and breaking out in a cold sweat.) The other universal triggers we all share are not yet known. Perhaps prayer is one of them.

CHAPTER 3
Doctors and Divine Healing

❧ ❧ ❧

Polls indicate that comparatively few doctors believe in divine healing or take spiritual concerns into consideration in their dealings with patients. But the evidence is mounting that caring for the spirit as well as the body can reap valuable health dividends. Each of us can benefit from the growing awareness of the power of faith among health care professionals. In this chapter we will explore some ways for faith to play a role in your health care.

Surgical history was about to be made in the operating room at the Medical University of South Africa in Medunsa. Before he began his work, the renowned neurosurgeon Dr. Benjamin Carson paused as he always does—and prayed.

Carson was eminently qualified to be lead surgeon in the groundbreaking operation of separating 11-month-old Joseph and Luka Banda, who since birth had been joined at the head. As chief of pediatric neurosurgery at Johns Hopkins Hospital in Baltimore, he had earned a worldwide reputation for pioneering innovative surgical techniques.

Carson had come out of a childhood of poverty and was committed to giving his time and talent to those less fortunate. And so it was that in 1997 he led the team of American doctors to South Africa to perform the operation on Joseph and Luka.

But 19 hours into the operation, it looked as if the chances of giving Joseph and Luka separate lives were diminishing. As the surgical team took a much-needed break, Carson wondered aloud if they should simply consider the case hopeless and close the babies' skulls. No one would question them if they were to abort the operation. After all, 13 previous attempts at this kind of separation had failed.

As Carson contemplated the dreadful decision that only he, as the leader of the surgical team, could make, he remembered sadly what had happened three years earlier. One of those 13 failures had been his.

Somehow the team found the strength to continue. In his book, *The Big Picture,* Carson writes, "As we walked back down the hall to the operating room, I began praying desperately that God would take over and simply use me to accomplish what only he could do."

Two verses from the Gospel of John came to mind as Carson, a devout Seventh-Day Adventist, prayed: "Very truly, I tell you, the one who believes in me will also do the works that I do and, in fact, will do greater works than these, because I am going to the Father" (14:12).

> As we walked back down the hall to the operating room, I began praying desperately that God would take over and simply use me to accomplish what only he could do.

Carson says he was emboldened to claim success in the operation because of what Jesus said. "Since the Scriptures don't tell about Jesus ever separating Siamese twins, I thought this probably qualified as one of those 'greater than these' things he promised we could do," Carson explains.

And succeed they did. After another grueling nine hours on the operating table, Joseph and Luka Banda were separated—and alive.

A few days later, with the Banda infants stabilized, Carson and his team were on a flight back to the United States. Seeing the newspaper headlines hailing the successful operation, Carson was filled with emotion. "I felt like serenading my fellow passengers with my own rendition of Handel's 'Hallelujah Chorus' in thanksgiving," he writes.

Despite being one of the most successful surgeons in the country, with a huge demand for his extraordinary skills, Carson is committed to his humanitarian projects, which he generously funds. "I think the concept of self-ishness is self-destructive and erosive for anybody," says Carson. "So you can only do yourself a favor when you give back because you can't out-give the Lord."

WHAT POLLS TELL US
ABOUT DOCTORS

A USA WEEKEND poll showed that although 63 percent of Americans said doctors should talk with their patients about faith, only 10 percent said their doctors had actually done so. The same poll showed that 90 percent of physicians don't want to mix religion with medicine. It's not surprising—research shows that fewer than half of all medical doctors feel close to God.

This patient–doctor dilemma is vividly illustrated in a 1991 study of Vermont family practitioners and their patients. Study results showed that only 64 percent of the doctors believed in God, compared to 91 percent of the patients. Only 45 percent of the doctors believed in an afterlife, compared to 60 percent of the patients. And approximately 60 percent of the doctors prayed regularly, compared to 85 percent of the patients.

How do psychiatrists and psychologists feel about faith and healing? When Gallup polled members of the American Psychiatric Association about their spiritual beliefs, 57 percent responded that they had none. When Gallup asked psychologists and psychiatrists if they agreed with the statement, "My whole approach to life is based on my religion," about two-thirds of each said no.

Some members of the mental health profession have actually referred to religious faith as an illness. This attitude may be traced back to the renowned psychiatrist Sigmund Freud, who said, "Religion is comparable to a childhood neurosis." Freud called religion a "universal obsessional neurosis"—a mental illness that afflicts virtually the entire human race!

While many in the mental health profession adopted Freud's opinions, some of the 20th century's most brilliant scientists thought otherwise. Nobel Prize–winning physicist Albert Einstein said, "Science without religion is lame; religion without science is blind." In his day a small but outspoken number of physicians and other scientists agreed. Today their numbers are growing, as many doctors see firsthand how faith works and can no longer ignore its potential. These doctors are learning how to use faith—their own as well as their patients'—to aid in healing.

> Nobel Prize–winning physicist Albert Einstein said, "Science without religion is lame; religion without science is blind."

CHOOSING A
HEALTH CARE PROVIDER

We can all benefit from the growing awareness of the power of faith among health care professionals. If you'd like faith to play a role in your health care, here are some ways to make it happen.

Be prepared. Talk to your family members and friends about their experiences with faith and healing. Take every opportunity to learn about people and treatments that embrace both faith and medicine. Begin looking for the right healers for you. And remember—the best time to begin looking for a doctor is when you're healthy—not when crisis strikes.

Be choosy. Select a healer carefully. A friendly personality and a willingness to pray with you may not be enough. You want a combination of good faith and good medicine. Ask people you know, especially those who share your faith, if they can recommend a doctor. Find out how that doctor brings faith into his or her medical practice.

Choose a doctor who treats you like a person, not a disease. In *Peace, Love & Healing,* Bernie S. Siegel, M.D., writes, "Doctors who persist in thinking they can cure the disease without caring for the person may be excellent technicians, but they are incomplete doctors, because they have an incomplete understanding of illness." Treating you like a person means, at the very least, listening to you attentively and respectfully.

Try to choose a doctor whose commitment to the role of faith in healing matches your own. One good way to find out where the doctor stands is by bringing up some of the studies you've read about. If the doctor responds enthusiastically and adds his or her own experiences with faith and healing, you've struck gold. If the doctor becomes uncomfortable or condescending, thank him for his time and look elsewhere. Each of us should feel free to express our beliefs and be treated with respect. And just as doctors should respect your beliefs, they also should not press their own beliefs on you.

> Try to choose a doctor whose commitment to the role of faith in healing matches your own.

In his book *A Physician's Witness to the Power of Shared Prayer*, William Haynes, M.D., of the Medical Center at Princeton, describes the gradual process through which he brought his faith into his medical practice. He began

by telling patients at the time of their release from his care that he had been praying for them. He writes that "this took great courage on my part because of the unorthodoxy of prayer as an adjunct to the standard medical treatment. Just the thought of mentioning it was frightening."

Haynes then began telling his hospitalized patients that he was praying for them. Only several months later did he begin asking patients if they would like him to pray with them. His offer of shared prayer, he reports, has never been turned down.

It's important to realize that your doctor may be waiting for you to make the first move. Some doctors listen for the language of faith in their patients' conversation and respond accordingly. That way, they don't have to worry about pushing faith where it's not wanted. Your doctor has no way of knowing at the outset if you're a believer or a nonbeliever. Don't be afraid to send your doctor a signal by mentioning faith in the conversation. You might tell the doctor that you are praying for healing or that your friends and family are praying for you. It may be just the opening the doctor is looking for.

Be involved. Although it is perfectly reasonable to want your doctor to acknowledge your faith, it is not

Honor physicians for their services,
    for the Lord created them;
for their gift of healing comes from the
        Most High,
    and they are rewarded by the king.
The skill of physicians makes them distinguished,
    and in the presence of the great they are
        admired.
The Lord created medicines out of the earth,
    and the sensible will not despise them. . . .
And he gave skill to human beings
    that he may be glorified in his
        marvelous works.
By them the physician heals and takes away pain;
    the pharmacist makes a mixture from them.
God's works will never be finished;
    and from him health spreads over all
        the earth.

❧

SIRACH 38:1–8

reasonable to expect him or her to be responsible for your spiritual well-being. That's your job.

If you are satisfied with your spiritual life, great. If not, you are probably aware of areas you would like to strengthen. Maybe you have faith but aren't part of a faith community. Faith grows when it is shared. And, as the research shows, participation in a community of believers is one way to unleash faith's healing power. It's not always easy to find your spiritual home, so don't be afraid to visit different groups. Ask questions and express your needs. And, by all means, pray for guidance!

Maybe you're just not comfortable participating in a religious group. Many people feel that they don't even know how to pray. Shared prayer intimidates nearly everyone at first. Ask a member of the clergy for encouragement, guidance, and good books about prayer. If you know someone who is very comfortable with prayer, ask that person to share what he or she has learned about it—and to pray with you.

If you see weaknesses in your own spiritual life, reach out for help in strengthening those areas. Spiritual wholeness is its own reward. Better health is just one of the fringe benefits.

Be yourself. If you want your doctor to treat you like a person, you have to let him or her get to know you as a person. Be open and honest, not only about your religious beliefs, but about your life and health. In *Peace, Love & Healing*, Siegel tells the story of a patient named Jake who had a brain tumor. "When the surgeon came down the hall Jake reached out to shake his hand, but

---

Maimonides' Oath for Physicians

❧ ❧ ❧

The eternal providence has appointed me to watch over the life, and health of Thy creatures. May the love for my art actuate me at all times; may neither avarice nor miserliness, nor thirst for glory or for a great reputation engage my mind; for the enemies of truth and philanthropy could easily deceive me and make me forgetful of my lofty aim of doing good to thy children. May I never see in the patient anything but a fellow creature in pain.

—THE 12TH CENTURY JEWISH PHYSICIAN/THEOLOGIAN MAIMONIDES

the surgeon pulled his hand back. Jake thought that the surgeon might be trying to protect his hands, so he then asked for a pat on the head instead. But the doctor again pulled back, saying that they were running late and needed to get to the operating room. At that point Jake roared, 'I refuse to have this man work on me! If he won't shake my hand or pat my head, I'm not letting him go into my brain!'"

Siegel goes on to say that studies show that patients who ask a lot of questions and maintain their individuality have stronger immune systems and better survival rates than submissive patients.

> Studies show that patients who ask a lot of questions and maintain their individuality have stronger immune systems and better survival rates than submissive patients.

Not everyone has the freedom to choose his or her doctor. In some cases, insurance companies may require policyholders to choose from an approved list of physicians. You may be hospitalized and have to deal with several medical specialists. At such times, it's easy to give up and give in. But if you have questions, ask them. If you're angry, say so. Pray, sing, and shout "hallelujah" should the occasion arise. Surround yourself with the support of fellow believers: friends, family, clergy. And remember to be yourself and keep the faith.

WHAT SCIENCE SAYS

There is more and more reason to shout "hallelujah" these days, as the results of scientific studies on faith are published. And they are exciting! Study after study affirms that faith is good medicine, says Dr. Dale A. Matthews, a professor of medicine at Georgetown University School of Medicine, a senior research fellow at the National Institute for Healthcare Research, and a practicing internist. In an issue of *Mind/Body Medicine* devoted to spirituality and medicine (Vol. 2, No. 1, 1997), Matthews writes, "When studied scientifically, religious commitment has been generally found to have significant health benefits. In a review of more than 200 published studies of the linkage between religion and health status, 75 percent revealed a positive relationship."

A strong sense of faith—combined with religious involvement—can result in better overall physical health, fewer and less severe symptoms, prevention of serious diseases including heart disease and cancer, less reliance upon the health care system, and better recovery when serious illness does occur. Faith is also linked to better emotional health. People of faith tend to be happier and more satisfied with their lives and relationships, and they tend to have higher self-esteem. Faith also helps to alleviate some mental health conditions, including depression and anxiety. Clearly, there is healing power in faith.

Writes Matthews in *Mind/Body Medicine*, "I do not encourage or demand patients to practice religion simply because I am a religious person and believe, as a matter of faith, that religion is good for your health (although both of those statements are true). As a believer in the scientific method, an orthodox medical practitioner, and a medical school professor, I believe that the medical value of faith is not a matter of faith—but of science. The scientific evidence of the health benefits of religious practice justifies its consideration in medical practice."

CHAPTER 4
Hope Springs Eternal

❦ ❦ ❦

Sooner or later, sickness or serious injury will visit each of us. And it will pay a call on those close to us as well. The question is not *if* we will receive the dreaded phone call late at night, but *when* tragedy will strike. But faith and hope are powerful resources to help us in our time of trial. If we learn how to tap into them, we will be able to find a blessed serenity when we need it.

ℬ ℬ ℬ

Late one night in April 1991, the lives of Darlene Bleich and her family were turned upside down. Earlier in the evening Darlene had a pleasant talk with her daughter Sherry, who was away for her first year of college. When they hung up, Sherry told her mother she was studying in her dorm room. At 11:30 P.M., just when it seemed that another uneventful evening was coming to a close, the phone rang.

"Why would Sherry be calling back now?" Darlene wondered. She was not prepared for the shock of hearing a deep voice on the other end of the line, informing her that her daughter had just been in a serious motorcycle accident.

Her mind reeling, Darlene could only think, "They're wrong!" But when the officer said, "Right now she's being taken by the Staff For Life helicopter to the trauma center at the University of Missouri Hospital," Darlene was jolted back into reality.

Rushing to the hospital, Darlene and her husband faced hours of emotional agony as they waited to find out whether their daughter would live or die. Incredibly, despite the terrible uncertainty, Darlene and her husband were encompassed by a peace that defied explanation—

Footprints in the Sand

❧ ❧ ❧

One night a man had a dream. He dreamed he was walking along the beach with the Lord. Across the sky flashed scenes from his life. For each scene he noticed two sets of footprints in the sand: one belonging to him, and the other to the Lord.

When the last scene of his life flashed before him, he looked back at the footprints in the sand. He noticed that many times along the path of his life there was only one set of footprints....

This really bothered him, and he questioned the Lord about it: "Lord, you said that once I decided to follow you, you'd walk with me all the way. But I have noticed that during the most troublesome times in my life, there is only one set of footprints. I don't understand why, when I needed you most, you would leave me."

The Lord replied: "My son, my precious child, I love you and I would never leave you. During your times of trial and suffering, when you see only one set of footprints, it was then that I carried you."

—AUTHOR UNKNOWN

The Story Behind "Footprints in the Sand"

❧ ❧ ❧

The beloved poem that has inspired millions, appearing on greeting cards, plaques, T-shirts, and postcards, is usually signed "Author Unknown."

But according to singer-songwriter Kathy Bee of Bellflower, Texas, the writer is no longer a mystery. Bee not only claims to know the author of the poem, she says she has a dated original copy.

The torn and faded handwritten poem in Bee's possession is dated 1939 and signed "Mary Stevenson." Bee met Stevenson after a performance in North Hollywood, Texas, in 1979. Stevenson, who was in the audience, struck up a conversation afterward and invited Bee to her home for dinner.

At Stevenson's house, Bee noticed a copy of "Footprints in the Sand" hanging on her wall. When Bee mentioned that she liked it, Mary went into a bedroom and brought out a box with hundreds of poems. Inside was a copy of "Footprints" from 1939.

Stevenson, who says she is a descendant of Robert Louis Stevenson, told Bee the story of how, as a poor and abused 14-year-old, she wrote the poem on a piece of scratch paper in 1936 while locked outside in the cold on the front porch of her childhood home in Chester, Pennsylvania.

As a young girl Stevenson had never thought about copyrights. She just enjoyed sharing "Footprints in the Sand" and other poems, passing out hundreds of handwritten copies.

Bee did all she could to publicize the woman she is convinced is the author of the poem. Later, author Gail Giorgio wrote a book by the same name that chronicles Stevenson's difficult life.

Over the years, challengers to Stevenson's authorship have included a Canadian woman who claims to have written the poem in 1964. However, several other earlier copies of the poem have turned up, substantiating Stevenson as the author.

Shortly before Stevenson's death in 1999, Bee paid tribute to her friend. "Mary has the greatest faith I've ever seen," Bee says. "It's a childlike faith, and I believe it has kept her alive."

a peace that could only have come from God—that night and throughout the difficult days that would follow.

Sherry's condition stabilized, but she remained in a coma. Tests revealed she had suffered a major head injury, but her family had to wait weeks to learn the full extent of the damage to her brain.

The next few weeks inched by as the Bleich family virtually lived by Sherry's bedside, watching for any small response: a faint squeeze from her hand, a sign of recognition in her eyes. Like countless others attending comatose loved ones, the Bleich family clung to any bit of hope. They seized on every possible response, wondering if each movement was real or imagined.

They strengthened their hope by hanging a large sheet of paper so that Sherry's visitors could leave messages of love and encouragement. Darlene kept a journal for each of Sherry's daily activities, recording every bit of progress—and each setback.

Day by day the Bleich family's hopes and prayers were being answered. As Sherry gradually improved, Darlene was reminded of the poem "Footprints in the Sand," which was a penetrating image of her daughter's experience. She imagined Sherry being carried along by the Lord through her darkest moments.

As Sherry was gradually restored to health, her family saw her develop a deeper spiritual awareness. This awakening led her to become sensitive to other people's needs, and she demonstrates limitless compassion and love. To share her newfound love for others, Sherry has volunteered as a bell ringer for the Salvation Army. But she wasn't content to simply ring her bell; she serenaded shoppers with Christmas carols, sometimes attracting small crowds who would pause to listen.

Today Sherry is a happily married mother of a little girl. There's no doubt she has come a long way since her accident, and she does not hesitate to give all the glory to God for her recovery. Proverbs 16:3 is a Bible verse that gives her inspiration to forge ahead: "Commit to the Lord whatever you do and your plans will succeed."

THE MANY FACETS OF HOPE

When the dreaded call in the night comes or illness befalls you or your loved ones, hope can be your mainstay. Hope is putting faith into action, demonstrating confidence that God is working on the situation. That is what Sherry's family was doing when they cheerfully decorated her hospital room and chronicled each tiny step of progress.

Hope is one part belief and one part attitude; it's a mixture of perseverance and surrender. And hope is there for the asking—you don't have to be born with it, you don't have to pay for it, and you never have to run out of it. In other words, hope springs eternal. Did you know hope can heal? Indeed, if you know how to use it, hope can be strong medicine.

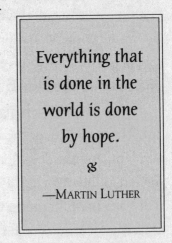

Everything that is done in the world is done by hope.

&

—MARTIN LUTHER

Throughout all ages and cultures, as long as men and women have faced the hardships of life, there has been hope. It is the irrepressible optimism that impels the survivors of war to rebuild shattered cities, families to continue their lives after crushing disaster, and patients to persevere when even the doctors have given up.

Hope manifests itself in different ways—depending on how much fear and uncertainty is present. Everyone likes to experience the kind of strong, confident hope that makes us feel lighthearted and excited. Most of us have also experienced desperate hope, which can cause a pounding heart, sweaty palms, and a feeling of uneasi-

ness. These emotional qualities of hope may be largely responsible for hope's powerful effect on the body.

Like faith, the importance of hope in the healing process has caught the attention of the medical world. Research shows that hope can help people survive all types of challenges—including terminal diseases. Perhaps that's why hope springs eternal in the human heart.

Hope Trusts in God

Doctors are not infallible. We have every right to hope to defy the odds our physician gives us, to seek a second medical opinion and possibly choose a different treatment than the doctor recommends, and to manage our illness and life in the way that best suits us.

But we cannot defy God. In *Peace, Love & Healing*, Bernie S. Siegel, M.D., writes, "... you have to know what to fight for and what to leave to God. Your rights and your individuality are things you owe it to yourself to fight for, by saying that you will not be a doormat, by insisting that your doctor treat you with respect, by making sure you get answers to your questions, by wearing your own clothes in the hospital, by participating in decisions that need to be made about your treatment. But there are other times when you must have faith and trust, when you must allow God to handle the burden so that you can be at peace. This combination of a fighting spirit and a spiritual faith is the best survival mechanism I know."

It seems the older we get, the more we remember our childhood. Many of us can remember the security we felt as children, when we depended upon our parents to feed, clothe, and protect us. At the time we didn't give it much thought. We simply expected our father and mother to take care of our needs.

In the same way, we need to rest in our childlike faith, to let God "handle the burden." This is not at odds with exercising strong, expectant hope. The basis of such a hope is faith that God can and will work miracles.

Hope Is Confident

Would Sherry Bleich be restored to health now if her family didn't stubbornly refuse to give up, marking every tiny sign of progress in her hospital room? Hope is eternally and unquenchably optimistic. It is the unwavering belief that, one way or another, things will be all right. Hope not only has a plan "A," but also a plan "B," "C," and "D." When plan A doesn't work out, hope begins working on plan B. Based on a strong conviction that

God is in control, hope is the expectation that *somehow* life will get better. With hope, things aren't as bad as they seem: There are always possibilities, options, and alternatives. But hope is always seasoned with uncertainty: We can only glimpse "through a glass darkly" the divine plan for our lives.

Although hope is influenced by circumstances and the people around us, ultimately it is an individual choice. A person who has chosen hopelessness can't be forced to have an optimistic outlook. Hope can be given only to those who are willing to receive it.

Once there was a man who hoped to have his own business, but twice he failed. At the age of 27, he had a nervous breakdown. Picking himself up, he decided to run for public office. He ran for office eight times, and eight times he lost. At the age of 51, the greatest hope and dream of this tall, gangly, and determined man finally came to pass. Abraham Lincoln was elected president of the United States.

Hope perseveres; it doesn't give up after one disappointment or two setbacks or three failures. In fact, it may be so bold as to try again for something even bigger.

Research shows that those with a stalwart, indomitable hope stand the best chance of healing.

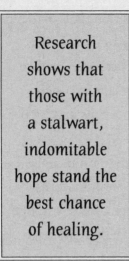

Research shows that those with a stalwart, indomitable hope stand the best chance of healing.

The British medical journal *The Lancet* reported a study of 57 women who had breast cancer. The study found that the women who responded to their cancer with a "fighting spirit" were more likely to be alive and cancer-free five years after their diagnosis than women who accepted the diagnosis stoically. (In fact, acceptance of the disease was actually found to be a sign of hopelessness.) Ten years after the women were diagnosed, 70 percent of the "fighters" were still living, compared to 20 percent of the patients who were resigned to their illness.

Hope Inspires Us

No doubt the determination of Sherry's parents was a powerful motivation for her recovery. The encouragement of others serves as a catalyst for our healing. It gives us the energy and the will to try to struggle against adversity. "Hope functions as a foundation for dealing with life and guides one's actions," writes Tone Rustøen, a registered nurse in Oslo, Norway, in *Cancer Nursing*.

"Strong hope gives strength and courage to press forward in handling difficult situations."

Survivors of the Nazi death camps in the Second World War say they could tell which of their fellow prisoners would be next to succumb to the inhuman conditions. They would become apathetic, losing all interest in the fight to survive. They had lost hope.

Similarly, why would anyone endure chemotherapy, with all its unpleasant side effects, without hope that out of the suffering will come healing? Those who persevere through months of painful physical therapy do so in the expectation that through the pain, restoration will come.

We must be careful not to confuse a hopeful, determined attitude with denial. Denial is the first of several stages that many patients go through after they are diagnosed with a serious illness. Most patients go through this stage, but a few get stuck there. Patients trapped in denial have difficulty committing themselves to needed treatments and life changes. They refuse to believe that they have a serious or life-threatening condition. What's more, denial prevents the activation of inner resources such as hope that can help fight a serious disease.

But determination is different. Denial says, "I'm not sick." Determination says, "I'm sick, but I'm not going to let it conquer my spirit. I'm going to fight it as best I can—and I plan to win." That's the kind of hope that offers the best chance at healing.

Hope Adapts to Changing Circumstances

One of the most useful qualities of hope is that it enables us to (more or less) cheerfully adapt to changing circumstances. Those lacking a hopeful attitude are often rigid and inflexible, and they have great difficulty in coping with the vicissitudes and misfortunes of life. Hope enables us to change our focus as circumstances change. Despite our best efforts at maintenance and prevention, our body will eventually deteriorate and perish. All human beings must die; there comes a point when it is no longer reasonable to expect a full recovery. Thus, our focus may shift. We may choose to use the time remaining to restore broken relationships or to leave a legacy of love for those close to us. As long as there is life, there is a purpose for our existence.

Hope Is a Shock Absorber

If you've ever had the shocks fail on your car, you know how rough the road can suddenly become. That's because there no longer exists a buffer between your posterior and the pavement. Similarly, hope is a coping mechanism that serves as a buffer against stark emotional realities. It helps us handle the minor and major crises of everyday life.

When the test results that we dreaded come back, hope for successful treatment kicks in. The higher the stakes, the more intensely we hope; if we didn't, we'd sink into a bottomless despair. As Tone Rustøen writes, "Hope is not normally present in a person's consciousness. It reaches consciousness when one is faced with a crisis or a conflict, like getting a cancer diagnosis."

Hope Draws From the Past

People who have been sick for a long time sometimes forget what it was like to be well. They see themselves only as sick. Ultimately, their whole lives—their thoughts, activities, and goals—revolve around their illness. As time goes by, they forget to hope for a healthier future.

We think of hope as being about the future, and mostly, it is. But hope also lives in the present and reaches into our past. Happy memories are an effective antidote to hopelessness. Positive memories allow a person to remember what it was like to be healthy, which sparks hope that they can be healthy again.

Hope uses light from the past to brighten present darkness and illuminate the future. "Remembered wellness," a term coined by Herbert Benson, M.D., author of *Timeless Healing*, refers to the practice of remembering times of health and happiness to help our bodies recapture and recreate that health. Hope is an important part of remembered wellness. Hope gives us the goal of regaining what once was and what can be again. Hope reminds us that this, too, shall pass.

HELPING HANDS INSPIRE HOPE

Despite how independent-minded we may be, the adage "No man or woman is an island" applies to all of us. Family, friends, doctors, nurses, and therapists all affect a person's ability to hope for healing. An article appearing in *Professional Nurse* quotes a patient as saying, "Other people influence my hope by their willingness to share a part of themselves through their affirmation, reassuring presence, encouragement, willingness to listen attentively, to touch, and to share hopes and feelings."

The doctor's role. We've been taught to believe that doctors are infallible experts, and we are usually inclined to believe what they say. While physicians are indeed highly skilled technicians who can save and prolong our lives, we can also be influenced by their attitudes. Doctors can either impart a sense of hope—or despair—in the patient.

Hippocrates, the ancient Greek physician, understood the influence that doctors have on their patients. "Some patients," he wrote, "though conscious that their condition is perilous, recover their health simply through their contentment with the goodness of the physician."

Siegel, too, understands his role in offering patients hope. In *Peace, Love & Healing* he writes, "Perhaps more powerful than any visualization or other specific technique you can use to alter the inner environment of your body are feelings of hope and love. I consider it my job as a doctor to give my patients both, because that's what they need to be able to live. Since I don't know what the outcome will be for any individual, no matter what the pathology report says, I can in all honesty give everyone hope."

Knowing how fully a patient is going to recover, or when a patient might die, is beyond the ability of any doctor. When they say that a patient will likely live a certain amount of time, they are relying upon a statistical average. But such averages contain a wide degree of variance. Doctors know what a disease can do to a person. What they don't know is how any particular individual may react to a disease.

Doctors have a responsibility to be forthright and honest with their patients who are gravely ill. But is it possible to inform a patient truthfully about a serious diagnosis and still leave the patient with something to hold on to in the form of sustaining hope?

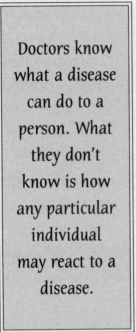

Doctors know what a disease can do to a person. What they don't know is how any particular individual may react to a disease.

"I have been with cancer patients at the time of diagnosis. I recall one circumstance in particular. I listened to a physician as he told the truth. He put it in the form of a challenge rather than a death sentence," writes Norman Cousins in *Head First: The Biology of Hope*. "He was not telling less than he knew; neither was he telling more than he knew. In his medical journals he had read of hundreds of unexpected remissions. And so he didn't feel under any obligation to provide any terminal date nor would he have done so even if asked. He was wise

enough to know that some people confound all the predictions, and he didn't want to do anything or say anything that would have the effect of a hex on the patient."

The wise doctor whom Cousins writes about knew how to make room for hope even in the most grim of prognoses. Whether or not doctors agree with the treatment option patients choose to follow, they should express hope to them. In *Peace, Love & Healing*, Siegel tells the story of a woman who, when given a diagnosis of brain cancer and a 90-day death sentence, chose to go to a clinic in Mexico that specialized in laetrile, a nontraditional treatment. Laetrile is a substance derived from raw bitter almonds and apricot pits, which some believe to be effective against cancer.

The woman responded to the laetrile treatment, and after a year felt quite well and was going on with her life. Then she happened to run into the doctor who had given her the death sentence. He was shocked to see the woman alive and in such good health. When she told him laetrile had given her a new lease on life, the doctor forcefully told her that laetrile didn't work and that he could prove it to her. He didn't need to. The woman was convinced he was right—and she died later that night.

"If the power of belief has enabled something to work for someone," Siegel writes, "I'm not about to use the authority of my profession to destroy its benefits. I know that hope and faith can sometimes provide patients with options that extend their lives when conventional medicine can do nothing."

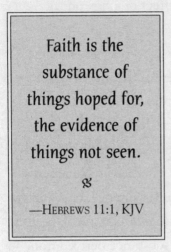

Faith is the substance of things hoped for, the evidence of things not seen.

⚮

—HEBREWS 11:1, KJV

Psychiatrist Karl Menninger, co-founder of the renowned Menninger Clinic, declared in *The Vital Balance*, "It is our duty as physicians to estimate probabilities and to discipline expectations; but leading away from probabilities there are paths of possibility, towards which it is also our duty to hold aloft the light, and the name of that light is hope."

Others instill hope, too. Doctors are not the only ones with a responsibility to encourage hope in patients. The words and attitudes of anyone a patient has contact with can have a strong influence on the patient's ability to hope. Parents must take care that they speak words of hope, not fear and despair, to their sick children. Family members and friends of a person who is ill can either add to, or subtract from, the person's store of life-giving hope. People can help keep hope alive for those who no longer have the strength to hope.

One day in February 1996, Alfredo Perez was teaching his elementary class at a Los Angeles school. It was a day like any other day until the shooting began outside his classroom. A moment later Alfredo lay crumpled on the floor, struck by a stray bullet that came through the window. Doctors told Alfredo's wife, Virginia, that he had zero chance for survival. When Alfredo defied their expectations and survived the initial trauma but remained unconscious for two months, doctors cautioned against hoping for more.

Exactly one year later, Alfredo and his wife appeared together at a news conference. Alfredo walked into the crowded room, followed closely by his wife, and spoke clearly and movingly of his recovery so far—and the healing yet ahead. Virginia Perez expressed her gratitude, saying that he couldn't have done as well without the doctors, nurses, physical therapists, and others. And she credited her husband for his determination, saying, "He never gave up."

Behind the scenes at the news conference, nurses told reporters that Virginia Perez had been at her husband's side every day for the past year. Perhaps it was she who brought him back to health—by giving daily and hourly doses of the hope he desperately needed.

The Perezes' experience is proof positive that none of us is ever beyond hope or too sick for a miracle. Where there's life, there's hope.

> Learn to focus on love. Try to make something very good out of something very bad. Try to live life in full fashion. I've seen people turn hurt into halos.
>
> §
>
> —REMARKS OF DR. PATRICK STAGG, ON NATIONAL CANCER SURVIVORS DAY

CHAPTER 5
The Healing Power of Hope

A split second, a screech of the tires, and the
sickening sound of sheet metal crumpling:
These can change your life forever. It happened
to Patricia Murphy one night on a highway in
Southern California. At 24, Patricia had a lot
going for her. She had graduated from
college with a pre-med degree and was
studying for the medical school entrance
exams. Her lifelong dream of a career
as a physician was within reach.

But all Patricia's plans were upturned along with her car as she was driving that evening to her second-shift job. A drunk driver smashed into her car. She suffered a head injury and severe whiplash, two disks in her spine were ruptured, and her left kneecap was smashed. Her ribs, nose, jaw, and several bones in her right hand were broken.

Doctors placed Patricia in a drug-induced coma to help prevent brain damage. After three weeks, she stabilized. But when she awoke from the coma, she didn't recognize her father. In fact, Patricia remembered almost nothing about her life before the car accident. Her speech was badly impaired, and she couldn't write.

Day and night followed one another in one long confused blur as Patricia drifted in and out of sleep. Awakening, she overheard a conversation outside her hospital room. Her father was telling one of the doctors that before the accident she had been about to enter medical school. "Well, she can forget about medical school," was the doctor's reply. Later, a neurologist and a psychologist would tell her father the same thing.

Doctors also told Patricia and her parents that she would never be able to take care of herself, hold a job,

> Hope is the best possession.
> None are completely wretched but those
> who are without hope, and few are
> reduced so low as that.
>
> ‿
>
> —WILLIAM HAZLITT

or become pregnant. "I refused to believe them," she says. "I told them I was going to medical school." Patricia's biggest worry, however, was that she had permanently forgotten all of her college education and that she'd have to repeat all the pre-med classes.

"I was a bad patient. I didn't take anything the doctors told me at face value. I questioned everything," she says.

Patricia's healing was slow and painful. For the next three years, she suffered from dizzy spells. For six years, as a result of the head injury, she suffered seizures. She even lost her driver's license for a period of time. But, despite her physical limitations, Patricia continued to work at various forms of physical therapy, trying to recapture her life before the accident.

Finally Patricia's speech returned to normal. She began to take control of her life. Despite her doctors' objections, when she stopped having seizures she insisted on gradually discontinuing her pain and seizure medications. She bought a house and moved into it alone—again, contrary to her doctors' advice. She enrolled in pre-med classes and was relieved to discover that she remembered most of the material.

It took nearly a decade of struggle and hard work, but in 1996, nearly a decade after the accident, Patricia declared herself fully recovered. She had defied the odds her doctors had given her. She was able to take care of herself. She was pregnant. And, on Christmas Eve, Patricia received a letter accepting her into medical school. She was thrilled, but not surprised. After all, she had never hoped for anything less.

HOPE—THE LIFESAVING OUTLOOK

Patricia's story is an encouraging reminder to hold on to hope and determination in the face of adversity. And her story is not the only one: For decades researchers have been studying the relationship between states of mind and their effects on healing.

In the 1940s, Caroline Bedell Thomas, M.D., tracked 1,300 medical students for 30 years, examining the link between psychological characteristics and physical health. Thomas found that people who had an unhappy childhood and kept their emotions bottled up were much more likely than others to get diseases such as heart disease and cancer. Less surprising, they were also much more likely to suffer depressive disorders and to commit suicide.

> If one prays and is convinced help is on the way, one is likely to try harder to actualize the desired outcome. Fantasy or not, prayer reinforces our own efforts and encourages us to make things happen. Those who pray, therefore, have an edge in the high-stakes game of survival.
>
> ❧
>
> —LARRY DOSSEY, QUOTED BY CHRISTINE STUTZ, "SPIRITUAL PRESCRIPTIONS: HOW PHYSICIANS, CLERGY, AND PATIENTS USE PRAYER AS A SOURCE OF HEALING," BALTIMORE JEWISH TIMES, AUGUST 28, 1998

At the same time, Harvard University was conducting a long-term study of 200 male students, investigating the link between their mental and physical health over a 40-year period. At the end of the study, the results indicated that mental health can have profound effects upon physical health. Of the 48 men with the worst mental health, 18 either had serious chronic diseases or were deceased. Of the 59 men with the best mental health, only two were seriously ill or deceased.

Researchers at the University of California studied the link between personality and disease in both AIDS and cancer patients. In cancer patients they found that traits such as compliance, conformity, self-sacrifice, denial of anger, and repression of emotion made a person less likely to do well. In their research on AIDS patients, they found that people who have

> People who have a sense of purpose, who take responsibility for their health, who express their emotions, and who have a sense of humor are likely to live longer than...people...who do not share these traits.

a sense of purpose, who take responsibility for their health, who express their emotions, and who have a sense of humor are likely to live longer than other people with AIDS who do not share these traits.

What Is Your Explanatory Style?

Research has proved that one's attitude can significantly impact one's health. Martin Seligman, Ph.D., a University of Pennsylvania psychologist, coined the term "explanatory style" to describe a person's mental and emotional response to stress and illness. It's the way people explain the events of their lives. Seligman studied the explanatory styles of 172 college students and was then able to predict which students would be sick a month later and a year later.

Life deals us certain cards, but how we perceive the hand we are dealt has a clear influence on our health. Two people, both of whom had an abusive childhood, can have two entirely opposite explanations for their early life. And these explanations will impact their health. The person who blames himself for the abuse, excusing his parents and believing that he brought the abuse upon himself because he was a bad person, leaves no room for hope. This person tells himself that he'll never accomplish anything worthwhile and will likely have poor health. Another person with a similar background might explain the abuse in a different way.

A hopeful person might say, "My parents were abused by their parents; they were repeating the bad behavior they learned. It had nothing to do with me, and I refuse to let it shackle me and my children." Such a person is more likely to live a healthy, productive life because he has succeeded in breaking the cycle of abuse.

In 1987, forty years after they began their research project, the Harvard researchers revealed eye opening findings about attitude: A man's explanatory style at age 25 could predict what his health would be like at age 65. They also found that the health of pessimists began to decline sharply at about age 45.

What a compelling advertisement for having a positive, hopeful outlook on life!

WHAT WE CAN DO

It takes more than hope to prevent or cure serious illness. Our emotional makeup and explanatory style, as well as our genes and environment, all play a part in determining who will get sick and who will recover. But while we cannot control our genes and have only some control over our environment, each of us can work on having a hopeful, positive attitude.

Judi Maiman was at rock bottom. After being in remission for six months following a terrible battle with pancreatic cancer, the doctors told her that three tumors had been found on her liver.

Throughout her bout with pancreatic cancer, the 59-year-old woman from Rockville, Maryland, had tried her hardest to maintain a positive attitude. But when she heard the terrifying diagnosis, she said she "fell apart" in her doctor's office. She told him she didn't think she had the strength to go through chemotherapy again.

If it were not for hopes, the heart would break.

§

—THOMAS FULLER, M.D.

"You cannot do this alone. You need God to help you," said her doctor, a devout Greek Orthodox Christian.

Her doctor's frank advice ignited a spark of hope in his Jewish patient. Judi went next to her rabbi for counsel. Friends and co-workers of varying religious

persuasions began praying for her. They encouraged her, refusing to let her abandon hope.

Judi summoned the courage to start another course of chemotherapy, and ten months later it seemed that her determination was paying off. Her CAT scans showed that two of the tumors had disappeared, and the third was shrinking.

Judi's healing is partic- ularly remarkable because pancreatic cancer is one of the deadliest forms of the disease. According to Dr.

> If you get healing of the soul, you get healing of the body.

Michael Auerbach, oncology chief at Franklin Square Hospital Center, chemotherapy for pancreatic cancer "does not appear to work."

Judi Maiman can't explain how prayer and hope have sustained her, but she's convinced they have, and that they're working.

Rabbi Mitchell Ackerson, chaplain at Baltimore's Sinai Hospital, writes: "If you get healing of the soul, you get healing of the body." Prayer "eases a person's psycho- logical suffering," he said, making it easier for them to address their physical illness.

And as we have seen, hope is one of the best healing balms for the soul.

Since we all need hope, and hope contributes to healthy living, where do we find that inner confidence that will help us live, thrive, and heal? Researchers have identified the following sources of hope among people facing health problems:

A Guiding Purpose

Probably more than any other single factor, having a sense of God-given purpose for our lives gives us hope to carry on, even in the face of terrible problems and circumstances. Knowing that there is a reason for our lives strengthens our will to overcome illness. This sense of purpose is often expressed in down-to-earth ways, such as being there to take care of the kids or watch the grandchildren grow. As anyone knows who has faced death or had a loved one face death, such "simple" things are really the most important of all.

This sense of one's life being held in the palm of God's hand can be very strong. It is not uncommon for those who have survived illness or accident to give as the reason that "it just wasn't my time." A person with a sense of purpose not only hopes but expects to be able to achieve his goals.

Writing in *Mind/Body Medicine*, Dr. Stephen G. Post, associate director of the Center for Biomedical Ethics at Case Western Reserve University, makes the connection between faith and hope: "Hope is the subjective sense of having a worthwhile future in the midst of anxiety," he says. "It is inherently relational and is usually mediated through religious ideation, symbol, practice, and community." People who have faith in a higher power have somewhere to turn in times of need.

> What's important is having people in our lives that we care about and who care about us. . . . And it doesn't matter if we have ten friends or two; quality is more important than quantity.

Supportive Relationships

The benefits of a strong, supportive family quickly become apparent when illness strikes. But where can people turn when they have no family support? This is

often the case for the elderly and those from broken homes. But they, too, can be filled with hope.

Besides their families, the most common sources of hope for older people are religious faith and friends in their social circle. These sources of encouragement are what give the elderly hope that they will be able to cope successfully with the challenges that come with aging.

Those who don't have supportive families can find hope and encouragement in long-time friendships. What's important is having people in our lives that we care about—and who care about us. We may know them from our work, or they may be our neighbors or friends from church. The good news is that it doesn't matter if we have ten friends or two; quality is more important than quantity. In addition, positive relationships with our health care providers can also be an important source of hope.

Reachable Goals

When you set a goal, you create a sense of hope. When you reach that goal, you hope to achieve new ones. This kind of hope can be a powerful ally in healing. Imagine a cancer patient who reaches her goal of being able to stay at the job she loves for one more month. When she

> People who believe they are courageous,
> resourceful, buoyant, and strong enough to
> endure suffering have confidence that these
> traits will be helpful in fighting illness.

attains that goal, she may be energized and encouraged enough to stay at work for another month, and another. Remember this Chinese proverb: A journey of a thousand miles begins with a single step.

A Positive Self-Image

When we are sick it's hard enough to feel good about ourselves without having to wrestle with self-image problems. People who already have a strong sense of self-worth are confident about who they are, their positive qualities, and their ability to persevere in times of trouble. When we look sick and feel sick, this solid sense of worth can provide a strong source of hope that, as before, we will once again be well.

Characteristics you like about yourself can be an important source of hope. People who believe they are courageous, resourceful, buoyant, and strong enough to endure suffering have confidence that these traits will be helpful in fighting illness. Conversely, people who lack confidence about coping with and triumphing over illness are not likely to have a successful outcome.

Laughter As Medicine

The ability to laugh and to maintain a lighthearted spirit are signs of emotional well-being, and they are good reasons for hope in overcoming illness. Laughter makes people feel better, both emotionally and physically. A good laugh can make us forget our troubles for a moment and put them in perspective. When we laugh, we remember that there's more to life than our pain, our disease, or our prognosis. Laughter and a sense of humor bring hope into the present by making us feel better even in the midst of suffering. And laughter can help us forget our fear.

A Hopeful Environment

Garbage in, garbage out, as they say. One of the ways to ensure a hopeful outlook is to fill our minds with positive, encouraging images. To find out what kind of images gave comfort and support to people, one study asked 12 people over the age of 65 to take photographs of things that gave them hope. Each of the 12 people took 12 photo-graphs over a one-week period.

Some of the photographs showed symbols and images of well-known, nearly universal sources of hope, such as churches and family members. But some of the pictures showed more personal choices. One participant took a photo of a mailbox, where she always hoped to find a card or letter from someone special. Another took a picture of the kitchen table, a source of familiarity and comfort. And one person took a picture of a clown, who gave hope for laughter and joy.

It is hope that maintains most of humankind.

❧

—SOPHOCLES

This study focused on an often-overlooked source of hope: our environment. And that's something we can control—at least to a certain extent. Think about how you feel after watching a movie with a violent or tragic story line compared with how you feel after watching a comedy or an inspiring story. The movies and television shows we watch, the books we read, the music we lis-ten to, and all the other sights, sounds, and objects that make up our environment can build or destroy hope.

In the New Testament's Book of Philippians, Paul wrote, "...whatever is true, whatever is honorable, whatever is just, whatever is pure, whatever is pleasing, whatever is commendable, if there is any excellence and if there is anything worthy of praise, think about these things" (Philippians 4:8). This is still good advice.

See the Beauty of Creation

God gave us the beauty of nature for us to enjoy—and to be a source of comfort and hope. Our world is turned upside down when we become seriously ill. When things suddenly go horribly wrong, nature can remind us that all of life is following a divine plan and that we are in the safest place—where God wants us to be—even though that may include suffering.

Autumn and winter are times when nature seems to fade and die. Leaves drop off the trees, animals hibernate or leave for a warmer climate, and even the sun seems to wane. It's easy to begin to lose hope as the world grows colder and darker, portending the rigors of winter.

But we survive the cold and the snow, and one day we notice a blade of green rising from the soil or a new bud forming on the seemingly dead limb of a tree. Spring cannot be stopped any more than winter can. The sun will rise as surely as it sets. God is in control not only of the world but also of what happens in our lives. Therein lies hope.

There are sources of hope other than those we have mentioned. Perhaps you have found your own special sources. Remember, anything that offers hope has the potential to heal.

THE ENEMIES OF HOPE

With so many sources of encouragement, why don't we continually radiate hope? The reason is, like all good things, hope has detractors, which can erode our positive outlook. Researchers have identified three factors that threaten to destroy hope in those who are suffering serious illness.

Loneliness

Suffering is magnified when we have to go through it alone. Those suffering from illness are often hospitalized and separated from family, friends, coworkers, and normal routines. Those who are in the time warp of a hospital ward can be painfully aware that outside life is going on without them.

Another reason isolation is a frequent side effect of long-term illness is that many people feel uncomfortable visiting the sick. They don't know what to say, especially when they are told that the illness is incurable. They fear emotional displays—either their own or the patient's. Some people stay away because of an irrational fear of catching illness just by being in a hospital.

Except for those fortunate to have strong family support that is present day in and day out, battling serious illness is a lonely struggle. The sick person suffers the pains of the illness, the side effects of the treatment, the life-and-death uncertainty—mostly alone.

To keep hope alive, there are steps that family, friends, and health care professionals can take to minimize these feelings of loneliness. If a friend or family member is hospitalized, make sure to visit the patient often. Talk about how much the sick

> There are no hopeless situations; there are only men who have grown hopeless about them.
>
> &
>
> —CLARE BOOTH LUCE

person is missed at home, work, or school. If the patient is at all able, make sure to get them out of the hospital. Plan outings; even a short trip to a nearby restaurant or a drive in the country can be uplifting.

If the patient cannot leave the hospital, why not bring the outside world to the patient? Friends and family can celebrate birthdays and holidays right in the hospital room. Don't be put off by concerns that

> If it is not possible to leave the hospital, why not bring the outside world to the patient?

it may be "inconvenient." Most hospitals are delighted to host celebrations of life and happiness, whether in the patient's room or in a special room set aside for such activities.

Misplaced Identity

One of the most difficult aspects of being sick is the near-total disruption of the familiar activities of one's life. Very sick people are usually unable to fulfill the roles that they typically play: Parents can't take care of their children or go to work, children can't go to school, and

grandparents can't spoil their grandchildren and participate in family activities.

The hospital routine adds to feelings of inadequacy
and insignificance when patients are helplessly shuffled
from one doctor to another and forced to endure endless
waits and painful procedures. Sterile, look-alike hospital
gowns erase each patient's unique personality. In such
an environment, it takes a strong personality to hold on
to one's individuality. But even individuals with strong
personalities may not feel up to the task when they're ill.

In *Peace, Love & Healing*, Siegel recommends that
hospital patients insist on wearing their own clothes
to help maintain a sense of identity. Most people are
unaware that this may be an option. He also suggests
decorating the hospital room to make it more personal
and comfortable—after all, you are paying for it! Do
whatever it takes to remind yourself—and everyone
around you—that you are an important human being
who deserves to be treated with respect, dignity, and
compassion.

Chronic Pain

Perhaps there is nothing that causes more stark fear
in those facing serious illness than the prospect of

uncontrolled, ongoing severe pain. Those suffering from painful disease or illness may not be able to sleep, think clearly, or perform routine tasks. They may become irritable and depressed, and they may also be ashamed that they have become like a child, requiring assistance for bodily needs. Some may try to escape from the pain by turning to alcohol and drugs. The physical and mental toll of chronic pain can quickly destroy hope.

Despite medical advances, doctors are sometimes unable to pinpoint the cause of the pain, making it difficult to treat. Pain is subjective, and our doctors can't put themselves in our shoes—or our hospital gown. Only the person suffering the pain can assess how truly bad it is. And medications don't work the same for all people. It may take some experimentation to find the right drug or dosage.

The alleviation of pain should be one of the doctor's top priorities. When dealing with chronic pain, it's important to have a compassionate physician who understands how devastating the pain is. And if the initial prescription doesn't take away the pain, the physician should readily substitute other medications and even be willing to try alternative approaches to pain relief. Family members and friends of people suffering from debilitating chronic pain should not hesitate to inquire on their loved one's behalf when the pain medication does not seem to be working.

Depression and Despair

We've all wrestled with it at one time or another, even if only for a fleeting moment. For those suffering from intractable illness, hopelessness can be a constant companion. And hopelessness is a negative, unsupportive, and pessimistic companion at that. The North American Nursing Diagnosis Association defines hopelessness as

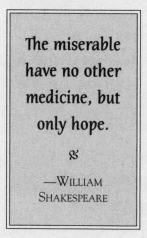

The miserable have no other medicine, but only hope.

§

—WILLIAM
SHAKESPEARE

"the subjective state in which an individual feels that alternatives and personal choices are limited or nonexistent, resulting in an inability to mobilize energy."

Like a friend who betrays us, sometimes the ones we look to most for encouragement can cause the deepest wounds. As unbelievable as it may seem, physicians who project hopelessness to their patients may see their expectation fulfilled. Some patients actually die because their doctors suggest they will. So, if ever a doctor hands you a death sentence, be sure to get a second opinion.

In *Head First: The Biology of Hope*, Norman Cousins relates the story of a woman who went to her doctor with an unexplained cough. After running some tests the doctor informed her that she had terminal cancer. He gave her a couple of months to live. The woman, who had been working and living a normal life, immediately stopped eating and started losing weight upon hearing the diagnosis. It looked like her doctor's prediction was right on target.

Somehow the woman had the presence of mind to get a second opinion. This doctor had a very different outlook. He told her that some people survived terminal

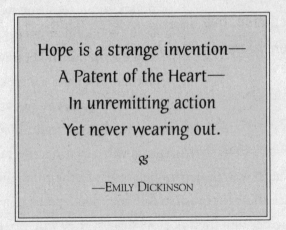

Hope is a strange invention—
A Patent of the Heart—
In unremitting action
Yet never wearing out.

&

—Emily Dickinson

diseases; he even introduced her to one person who had recovered from a disease similar to her own. The doctor recommended that she get the best possible medical treatment and use all of her inner resources—physical, emotional, and spiritual—to help her body heal. At the time when Cousins' book was published in 1989—long after the woman's 60-day death sentence—she still had cancer, but with hope, she was maintaining a good quality of life.

Doctors are often not aware of the impact of their words on their patients. What they say can often destroy any feelings of hope their patients may have. As an example, in *The Canadian Nurse*, Louise Niessen, R.N., tells this story of her mother's death from breast cancer. "My mother's method was to hold on to hope. Her relative peace of mind, however, was threatened more and more with each follow-up visit to the clinic," she writes. "Her decline was reinforced by what we perceived as cold and detached professionals, slowly chipping away at hope. Subliminal messages have negative results.

"When the cancer clinic could offer no further treatment for my mother, we were seen by a student doctor we'd never met. He told us that we could expect another month and that he was sorry if this was bad news. Our personal feelings of grief and disappointment were ignored."

Niessen concluded from this painful personal experience that the doctors were wrong in giving her mother's life a deadline. More than anything else, it was setting a deadline for her mother to die that stifled her ability to hope for recovery.

After watching doctors destroy her mother's hope, Niessen vowed to change the way she, as a nurse, relates to patients. "I will continue to listen to patients, as venting is a vital part of dealing with stress and anxiety," she writes. "In addition, though, I now offer the positive encouragement I was afraid to offer before. Hope is never wrong."

In addition to a pessimistic doctor, other factors that can literally be fatal for patients have been isolated by research. Hopelessness can make people sick, and it can keep them from getting well. In the 1950s, researchers at the University of Rochester identified three elements that resulted in what they called "the giving up–given up complex." The elements were hopelessness and helplessness, a poor self-image, and a lack of satisfaction from relationships and roles (such as being a parent, worker, volunteer, etc.). The researchers studied people with all kinds of serious illnesses and found that 70 to 80 percent of the patients had fallen into the giving up–given up complex before they became ill.

ANGELS OF HOPE

Have you ever met someone who exudes hope and encouragement? Carolyn Omang calls one such person her "angel." Carolyn and Dixie had been good friends and colleagues who had somehow drifted apart over the years as they both took different jobs. They tried to keep up but hadn't seen each other in months. Then one day Carolyn ran across Dixie in the pharmacy. It turned out that both of them were getting prescriptions filled: Carolyn for medication related to a recent surgery and Dixie to relieve symptoms of a vague, tiring illness.

Carolyn didn't have a car, so Dixie offered to drive her home. In the car Carolyn asked about Dixie's undiagnosed problem. "The doctors are running tests—you know how it goes," said Dixie, brushing off Carolyn's concerns. She thought it was probably stress related to her fast-paced job with a property management job at a Colorado ski resort.

Despite her best intentions, Carolyn didn't get together with Dixie after their brief encounter and only by chance learned several months later that Dixie's "vague illness" was terminal lymphatic cancer. She had as little as six months to live.

Carolyn was shocked and devastated. Memories came flooding back of their long friendship. She remembered when she returned to work after having minor surgery. She wasn't in the best of spirits, but Dixie changed all that when she walked in dressed up as "Miss Piggy," complete with pig nose, ears, and feather boa. Carolyn laughed so hard she nearly popped her stitches. Dixie was a natural comedienne, always smiling and laughing— even about the many trials of her own life.

No matter what the situation at work or in someone's personal life, Carolyn remembered that Dixie wouldn't let it get them down. When Carolyn was going through a painful divorce, Dixie showed up, bringing her lunch and some audiotapes on healing and relaxation. The tapes soothed Carolyn enough so that she was finally able to sleep and begin healing from her lost marriage.

"Carolyn," said Dixie, "whenever you're in a bad situation, always look for the lesson that can be learned from it. No matter how bad it is, there is always something positive to be learned."

But Carolyn couldn't find anything positive about Dixie's illness. Soon Dixie was in the hospital for the last time; it was apparent that she wasn't going home. Carolyn went to the hospital and saw her emaciated friend on her bed surrounded by tubes and bottles of medicine.

> In everyday life . . . we must hold ourselves in balance before all created gifts . . . we should not fix our desires on health or sickness, wealth or poverty, success or failure, a long life or a short one. For everything has the potential of calling forth in us a deeper response to our life in God. Our only desire and our one choice should be this: I want and I choose what better leads to God's deepening of [His] life in me.
>
> ❧
>
> —SAINT IGNATIUS, SPIRITUAL EXERCISES

Choking back tears, Carolyn summoned her courage and asked, "Dixie, you always told me to look for the lesson in a bad situation. What's the lesson here?"

Almost inaudibly, Dixie replied, "If it was for only one person, it was worth it."

"One person!" thought Carolyn in astonishment. Her life had touched so many.

A few weeks after that poignant visit, Carolyn was preparing for bed when suddenly she heard a loud flutter. She asked her husband if he had heard it. He hadn't.

"It sounded like a bird just flew past my head. It seemed to have such huge wings!" she said. Or was it an angel? The next day Carolyn received the news that her friend had died the day before—the same time that Carolyn experienced her "angelic" visit.

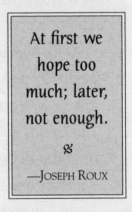

At first we hope too much; later, not enough.

⅋

—JOSEPH ROUX

A few days later at Dixie's memorial service, Carolyn read the note Dixie had written for her family and friends before she died: "This is not a tribute to my life, but to all of you, who have given me so much love. I thought my heart would burst with love for you. Thank you for

making my life beautiful! You have truly been the wind beneath my wings."

Carolyn was so moved by Dixie's life and testimony to the power of hope that she began volunteering to drive cancer patients who have no transportation to their chemotherapy appointments. She also took hospice training so that she can provide support for patients and care for families going through the process of losing a loved one.

The old adage is true: The more you give, the more you receive. Dixie poured out her heart and life seeking to cheer others, and in the end she was powerfully ministered to by those she had served. Her example can encourage us to "enlarge our borders" and be angels of hope to others. We in turn will reap a bounty of inner peace and contentment.

CHAPTER 6
Social Support and Healing

❦ ❦ ❦

Research shows that people who attend religious services enjoy more health benefits than those who don't. The benefits may include a decreased risk of coronary disease, emphysema, cirrhosis of the liver, and deaths from suicide. Some of those benefits can be attributed to the healing effects of social support. Whether it comes from a religious community, family and friends, or even from a pet, social support influences our emotional health. It can make a life-and-death difference.

In 1971 Gary Severson was a graduate student at the University of Washington. He was also a very sick man awaiting a kidney transplant. During the previous two years, he had been summoned nine times into Seattle's University Hospital for a possible transplant. For one reason or another, each time the "mission" was scrubbed.

Finally an acceptable donor kidney was found. The hospital admitted Gary as soon as he could scribble his signature. After seven-and-a-half hours, he awoke in his hospital room with a new kidney.

But it didn't function.

The doctors assured him that the kidney would probably recover shortly. As Gary sat in bed pondering his prospects, the hospital chaplain came in and gently asked if he could be of assistance.

"I'm sorry," replied Gary, "but I'm not interested in your religion. Have a good day, though." The chaplain didn't argue; he handed Gary his card and left, still smiling. *What some people do for a living,* thought Gary, disdainfully.

The chaplain wasn't so easy to forget, though, especially as Gary began experiencing setback after setback. Not only did his new kidney refuse to work, but his potassium level soared, and he could not raise his feet and legs from the bed. The medicine made his thinking muddled and cloudy.

Things got worse. He developed a bleeding problem with one of the tubes inserted in his body. The antirejection shots in his hip made Gary scream in pain, and his daily liquid-restricted diet, barely two cups, hardly wet his parched throat.

And still the kidney refused to function. As he continued to deteriorate physically, Gary became increasingly depressed and cynical. Friends stopped visiting; even the nurses seemed to avoid him.

Never mind—I'll make it without them, thought Gary defiantly. He'd pull through. He always had. But one evening, after a particularly hard day, he was listening to the radio when the deejay decided to play the song "The Old Rugged Cross" as a joke. Somehow Gary wasn't in the mood for his brand of humor. The song irritated him, and he turned off the radio in disgust.

Still, for a moment it had him thinking about God. Memories began flooding his mind, pictures of his boyhood spent in church with the pastor, praying behind the pew. Family and friends were once again around him, participating in the communal worship of believers. He saw himself reciting Scriptures for Sunday School and enjoying himself at church picnics. The vivid, moving images puzzled Gary. He'd left religion behind as soon as he was old enough to strike out on his own. Why the memories now?

Gary happened to glance in the mirror across the room and saw what he had become: a shriveled form with a vacant stare. He had the look of death. Shocked and terrified, he pressed his fingers to his hollow cheek as if in disbelief.

"God, why have you forsaken me?" moaned Gary. Despairing of his enfeebled existence, tired of suffering without a kidney, he determined to end it all. Gary dragged himself to the window ledge and tried to open the window to jump. He couldn't budge it.

He slid off the ledge and onto the floor, crying out in a whisper, "God, help me! I'll do anything! Please!"

> For a moment it had him thinking about God. Memories began flooding his mind, pictures of his boyhood spent in church with the pastor, praying behind the pew.

As Gary crawled back into bed, a gentle peace crept over him. The next day everything seemed brighter. Even the doctors and nurses seemed more cheerful. Then Gary realized that it was his outlook that had been transformed by his prayer the night before.

where Are the Believers?

❦ ❦ ❦

It appears likely that more people could benefit from a renewed interest in becoming part of a religious community. A Gallup poll found that, while 95 percent of Americans believe in God, only 42 percent regularly attend religious services. Why?

Not all people are rebels like Gary. Those who are old or infirm may not be up to attending services. Some people believe in God but are not committed to any particular denomination. Others haven't found a faith community in which they feel comfortable. And some simply can't find—or don't make—the time.

Was it my imagination, thought Gary, *or am I feeling better physically as well?* That question was answered the next day when he had a strange urge. For the first time since his operation, Gary needed to urinate. Gary reached for his urinal, realizing that his kidney had started functioning.

Elatedly, he dragged himself to the door of his room and waved the urinal in the hallway, yelling "I did it!"

Gary—or more accurately God—did it. That day his kidney had begun functioning. In the years since then, he has not experienced any rejection symptoms, even though the kidney he received was rated a "D" match— the worst match a transplant victim could receive at that time.

"Over the years, as I've gotten to know the Lord better," says Gary, "I've come to believe that there were two things within me in that hospital room: a kidney that was in place and not working, and the relationship with God that I had buried inside me since my youth. I tried to reject both, but neither rejected me. Now the continuing functioning of my kidney is a sign to me of God's faithfulness, mercy, and enduring love."

HOW A RELIGIOUS
COMMUNITY HELPS

As a desperately sick Gary lay in that hospital room, he was brought back to God by his childhood memories of church—the community of believers he had tried so hard to run away from. No one is suggesting that Gary would not have become sick if he had continued in church. But there is mounting evidence that participation in an organized religion or a faith community has positive health effects.

Of course, it's a personal decision to become part of a religious community. But research shows that people who attend religious services and events enjoy more health benefits than those who don't—in addition to whatever spiritual benefits are gained.

One of the first studies of the relationship between church attendance and health was reported in the *Journal of Chronic Disorders*. The study looked at death rates among nearly 92,000 people in one county in Maryland. There were fewer deaths among those who went to church every week than among those who attended services less frequently or not at all. Specifically, the weekly churchgoers experienced 50 percent fewer deaths from coronary disease, 56 percent fewer deaths from the lung disease emphysema, 74 percent fewer deaths from the liver disease cirrhosis, and 53 percent fewer deaths from suicide than the non-churchgoers.

A nine-year study of death rates in Alameda County, California, reported similar results. Church members had lower death rates than people who were not members of a church. Another study of women in Tecumseh, Michigan, found that those who attended church lived longer.

And, as it turns out, going to church can do a whole lot more than just increase your life expectancy. A study at Wayne State University in Detroit found that African American men who regularly attended religious services were less depressed, smoked fewer cigarettes, and drank less alcohol than their counterparts who didn't attend church services.

> **In healing communities, people are praying for each other, and it's all about fixing broken hearts. Hospitals are about fixing broken bones.**
>
> ❧
>
> —SISTER KAREN HELFENSTEIN,
> ST. VINCENT'S HOSPITAL, NEW YORK CITY

David Larson, M.D., president of the National Institute for Healthcare Research (NIHR), oversaw a study that tracked the blood pressure of 400 white men in rural Georgia for 30 years. The study found that churchgoers had lower blood pressure levels than people who did not attend church very frequently.

More recently, in 1996, Duke University psychiatrist Harold Koenig reported the results of a study by the National Institute on Aging. The study of 4,000 seniors in North Carolina found that those who attended religious services were physically healthier and less depressed than those who didn't. Interestingly, the study found that watching religious television and praying alone did not have the same health benefits as being part of a religious community.

The Theories

There are several theories about why participation in a religious community helps people stay, or become, healthy. Some researchers think churchgoers are healthier because the faith community provides a strong network of social, emotional, and spiritual support. Feelings of being isolated, alone, and uncared for are unhealthy;

any community or support group that prevents such feelings is bound to enhance health.

Other researchers suggest that participation in organized religion may be beneficial because faith communities are often places where many unhealthy behaviors are frowned upon. In the Wayne State University study, the churchgoing men likely smoked and drank less because smoking and drinking are not

> **Feelings of being isolated, alone, and uncared for are unhealthy; any community or support group that prevents such feelings is bound to enhance health.**

acceptable behaviors in most churches. Thus, going to church may be an effective method of behavior modification that leads to good health and long life.

In the Seventh Day Adventist church, most Seventh Day Adventists are vegetarians, nondrinkers, and non-smokers. Studies have consistently shown that Adventists tend to have longer life expectancies than the general population—nine years longer for men, four years longer

for women—and much lower rates of death from certain diseases.

Dale Matthews, professor of medicine at Georgetown University School of Medicine and senior research fellow at the National Institute for Healthcare Research, believes that the actual content of religious services can also have "measurable physiological effects." That is, congregational singing and praying actually may have a beneficial effect on physical health. According to Matthews, the religious service is a place to meet God and a place where God meets the needs of many people in various ways.

From Skeptics to Believers

Studies of faith's role in healing are beginning to impact the health care system. Yankelovich Partners surveyed doctors attending a meeting of the American Academy of Family Practitioners. Of 296 doctors surveyed, 99 percent said they believed that religious faith could heal; 75 percent said they believed that prayer could help people get well. These figures are much higher than would be expected, given results of past surveys that asked health care professionals the same types of questions. Clearly, something is changing their minds.

Medical schools, including the highly respected Johns Hopkins University, Ohio State University, and Penn State University, now offer courses and programs on spirituality and medicine. More universities are adding similar courses every year. Harvard Medical School has established a biannual conference called "Spirituality and Healing in Medicine."

> The more we learn about faith's medical prowess, the more we see mainline religious denominations returning to the healing fold.

Interestingly, it is not just the medical community but also the religious community that is responding to the research. "The more we learn about faith's medical prowess, the more we see mainline religious denominations returning to the healing fold," writes Herbert Benson, associate professor of medicine at Harvard Medical School, in his book *Timeless Healing*.

He notes that Andover Newton Theological School, among others, has put faith healing into its curriculum, and he quotes an official of the school as saying, "Healing was once a major part of the mission of the church but we abdicated it. We began to think that healing was a secular enterprise. But now, having become immersed in the study of mind/body connections, we realize we have a valuable role. We've become less self-conscious about it, that healing is part of the Christian tradition, that it isn't just a gimmick from a charlatan. Now faith healing is a central focus for us, and we hope to be at the forefront in teaching others about it."

Francis McNutt, a former Dominican priest, was an early leader in bringing the church back to its healing roots. McNutt and his wife, Judith, now head Christian Healing Ministries, an organization that helps local churches begin their own healing ministries.

The Jewish community, too, is reclaiming its role in healing. Some temples now offer healing services, and more and more Jewish congregations are interested in participating. Elat Chayyam, a Jewish "center for healing and renewal" in Woodstock, New York, holds a variety of healing workshops.

As both the medical and religious communities respond to early research, there is wide agreement that more studies are needed. Researchers are calling for long-term studies that clarify the results of the healing effects of prayer. Matthews is now conducting a carefully structured study in which people trained by McNutt are offering patients spiritual counseling and both verbal and nonverbal prayer (the laying on of hands).

SUPPORTED BY FAITH

Peggy Keleher is living proof of the role of faith in healing. Like Judy Maiman, Alice Andrews, and the others we've heard about, Peggy's diagnosis of cancer in 1965 hit her like a freight train. The anticipation of losing a breast wasn't the worst of it. In those days it was thought that the reproductive system was somehow connected with breast cancer, and as a precaution, surgeons routinely removed the ovaries along with the cancer.

Peggy was just 28. She and her husband Michael had three daughters, aged 1, 2, and 3. And they were looking forward to having more children.

A practicing Catholic who believed in God's power and love, Peggy sought the counsel of her priest as well as friends and family. Her two brothers, who were both doctors, accepted the conventional medical wisdom of the day and urged her to let the doctors take her ovaries, even though it meant never having another child.

Prayerfully considering all her treatment options as well as the input from those around her, Peggy decided

> Something we really wanted in life
> was a partner who would help us
> keep our faith and help it grow.

against any treatment that would make it impossible for her to bear children.

Thirty-five years and two girls and one boy later, Peggy is still alive and thriving. With their six children and nine grandchildren, she and Michael have the large—now extended—family they always wanted. Looking back, Peggy reflects: "Something we really wanted in life was a partner who would help us keep our faith and help it grow." Remembering the decision against the hysterectomy, she says: "At the time, it seemed like we were older. Here [Michael] was on the verge of having three daughters and possibly losing his wife." How did they survive? "Our faith is the secret of our success," say the Kelehers.

Peggy's personal faith was supported by those around her: first of all, her husband Michael, but also family, friends, and their church. Without their encouragement she might not have had the strength and determination

to make the decision she felt was best and stand up to her doctors.

BODY CHEMICALS AND EMOTIONS

Researchers are discovering that the mind and body are inextricably entwined and that, for better or worse, the emotional connections in our lives influence our health. Studies show that positive relationships with those around us lend the kind of support that can keep illness and death at bay. Those who have close, loving relationships tend to live the longest and healthiest lives.

We all have built-in physical mechanisms to help us cope with stress. These mechanisms are a significant part of the explanation of how social support—or the lack of it—influences our emotions and our health.

Most of us can still remember falling in love for the first time. Strange new emotions, at once euphoric and apprehensive, flooded us. Our stomach was tied up in knots at the fear of rejection, and we experienced rapturous heights of bliss when our love was reciprocated. Our face turned a blushing crimson, our palms got sweaty, and our pulse quickened.

These feelings are the result of chemical changes that occur in our bodies when we experience different emo-

What Love Has to Do With It

❦ ❦ ❦

Over the years, scientific studies of people who get sick and people who remain healthy have revealed many factors that have an impact on good health. Among them are the following:

- ❧ Being in love helps to protect against colds and strengthens the immune system.
- ❧ Touching patients helps them recover more quickly.
- ❧ Having relationships helps you live longer.
- ❧ Knowing you're loved helps you recover more quickly.
- ❧ Having a pet helps you survive disease.
- ❧ Talking to someone who listens can help you recover three times faster.

tions. Scientists have learned that the physical reactions that accompany our emotions can be traced to a class of chemicals in the brain known as endorphins. These endorphins (a type of neurotransmitter) can ease pain when we are hurt; they are also responsible for the natural "high" that people who exercise strenuously experience after completing a couple of fast laps around the track.

Endorphins also strengthen the immune system. When our endorphin levels are high, our immune system becomes stronger. As our endorphin levels rise, we get sick less often. And when we do get sick, a strong immune system helps speed recovery.

Studies suggest that our emotional connections with others also influence our endorphin levels. Gestures of emotional support—a touch, a hug, a smile—can trigger a burst of endorphins. Thus, each time we kiss our spouse or hug our child, these "feel good" chemicals are released. Emotional connections, then, help strengthen our immune system by stimulating the production of endorphins.

"Fight or Flight" and Stress

Our problem in the modern age may just be that we're no longer hunting mastodon in Northern Europe or wildebeests in the African savanna. Our brains still respond to stress by secreting hormones that allow us to respond to danger by either fighting or fleeing. These hormones were invaluable at one time: They literally saved our lives when an enraged prey suddenly turned to attack its hunter. There was no time to discuss various options—immediate, instinctual response took over. So the hunter either stood his ground and attempted to kill his prey or, if the beast was too powerful for him, turned tail and ran.

But these days the challenges and options we face are ambiguous. Few of us face mortal, external physical threats on a regular basis, as our ancestors did. Our dangers are more likely to be an unsympathetic boss who has the power to fire us at will or a disease that is ravaging our body. We have experiences that plunge us into despair, such as a poor relationship with a loved one or the loss of a life partner. And we have more minor crises, such as an argument with a spouse, a missed bill payment, or an overdue library book—all of which can trigger stress.

Even though we possess the same fight or flight mechanism as our prehistoric ancestors, we cannot simply physically attack and destroy what threatens or stresses us. Nor can we suppress the physical reactions to stress. The central nervous system responds to the "fight or flight" imperative by pumping "stress chemicals" through our body. Whatever the stressful situation, the result is the same: The body is flooded with these stress chemicals.

These chemicals have both positive and negative attributes. On the plus side, they are essential in mounting an effective response against severe stress due to disease or injury. They cause our heart to race and our blood pressure to rise. Sugar is released into the blood, increasing our metabolism.

Momentary bouts of stress don't seem to have a strong impact on the body. In most people, once the source of the stress is removed, the body's chemical levels go back to normal and all is well. We get over the argument or we pay the overdue bill, and our health improves. Our stress is relieved, we feel more relaxed, and our immune system suffers no permanent harm.

People who live in a continuous state of stress, however, are likely to suffer from the negative aspects of surging chemicals. They live in a constant state of arousal; their bodies are constantly ready to fight or flee. And they are overexposed to potent chemicals and hormones that can ultimately damage the body. This type of relentless stress can depress the immune system, making the body more vulnerable to disease. People who are depressed or bereaved, for example, often experience a gradual slowdown in immune function. Constant stress can also affect personality. Some individuals may feel tense and explosive while others feel hopeless or helpless.

Ultimately, the immune system loses much of its ability to fight disease. As the immune system continues to break down, the body begins to lose its battles with invading disease organisms. As a result, we become sick more and more often—thus causing even more stress.

How to stop this vicious circle? If we can intercept the stress-induced flood of chemicals, we will have a better chance of staying healthy. One way of doing this is to have healthy primary relationships and a solid base of social support—people with whom you can vent your concerns, frustration, and anger without fear of rejection.

You may believe that you don't have anyone like that in your life. But unless you live on a desert island, you have relationships with other people. And even though you may not be part of a formal religious community, God uses all kinds of people to minister to us. The key is to develop healthy, encouraging friendships. One sure way of doing this is to heed the biblical proverb: "The one who desires friends must prove himself to be friendly." Friendship is a two-way street that each of us can journey down, and we have the promise that our efforts will be rewarded.

RELATIONSHIPS AND HEALTH

Hundreds of thousands of people have been tracked by numerous studies over the past several decades to discover who gets sick and who doesn't—and what factors explain the difference. Researchers studied what the participants did for a living, what they ate and drank, and what their medical histories revealed. They looked at their good and bad habits, how much they exercised, and how much sleep they got. And, most revealingly, they looked at their families, their friendships, and whether they believed in God.

Researchers found that four types of social bonds affected longevity: marriage, contact with family and friends, church membership, and group affiliations. The researchers found that those who had the weakest social connections were twice as likely to die in the next nine years as those with the strongest ties. In fact, the relationship between social isolation and death is as strong as the relationship between smoking and death or high blood cholesterol levels and death.

Married People Are Healthier

For more than a hundred years, researchers have known that married couples have lower death rates from a whole range of different diseases than single people do. And the health of married people can't be explained away by assuming that people who get married—and stay that way—are just healthier to begin with. Researchers at the University of California at Los Angeles (UCLA) have found that, for a variety of reasons, it's the state of marriage itself that has the most impact on maintaining good health.

The Framingham Heart Study, which has tracked the health of 5,000 people for the past 30 years, found that getting and staying married is a predictor of a long, healthy life. Other studies reveal that people who lead isolated lives are two to three times more at risk of dying at a young age than are people who feel connected to

> How can a wedding band ward off disease? Reaching out to another human being has a measurable, positive physical effect within the body, boosting levels of endorphins and enhancing the immune system.

others. A study of more than 25,000 cancer patients found that married people were more likely to survive longer than single individuals. Married people were also more likely to have cancer diagnosed at earlier, more curable stages and to start treatment sooner. Even when members of the married group were diagnosed with cancer at more advanced stages, those who were married seemed to have the best odds for survival.

How can a wedding band ward off disease? Reaching out to another human being has a measurable, positive physical effect within the body, boosting levels of endorphins and enhancing the immune system. It's not just folk wisdom. People who are in love do have fewer colds. It stands to reason that, with more active immune systems, those who are married tend to be a lot healthier than those who are unattached. But there are other, very practical reasons why having a committed relationship is beneficial to health.

Being sick can be very overwhelming—especially if there's no one there to hold your hand, to speak up for you, or to ask questions when something doesn't make sense. Those undergoing cancer treatment, for example, face a battery of unfamiliar and frightening experiences. They'll need to make countless trips to the doctor and the hospital for tests and exams, drug treatment, or radiation therapy. Someone facing the terrifying reality of cancer can be so overwhelmed that just the effort of getting out of bed in the morning can be a Herculean task, and the side effects of some cancer treatments may leave you too exhausted to even try. And even if you are up to making the trip to the hospital to receive your treatments, if you live alone, you may not be able to drive yourself there.

Married people have a safety net of support that helps them better deal with stress and recover from illness. They have someone right there to help with keeping appointments, too. Married people also have a powerful incentive for getting better: Their spouse needs them. That sense of obligation to a life partner makes married people more likely to take their medicine and keep their doctor and hospital appointments—even knowing the unpleasant procedures that lie ahead.

Married People Live Healthier Lifestyles

If you're married, you won't just have an incentive to get better, you actually will be getting sick less. That's because married people typically lead a healthier lifestyle.

Single folks are more likely to grab fast food on the run or eat a pork chop standing over the kitchen sink because there's often no one to eat with. Who needs the hassle of going through the effort of preparing nutritionally balanced meals when there is no one to share them with? Married couples are much more likely to eat balanced meals at regular hours than are single people.

In addition to eating right, married couples also tend to lead more measured, traditional lives. When a man gets married, he is usually pleasantly surprised to find out that his auto insurance rates have dropped. And for good reason. Statistics show that attached men are less likely to be risky drivers.

Being married usually means you're a lot better off financially, too. In fact, studies by the Federal Reserve Board and Princeton University found that single men earn up to 50 percent less than married men of the same age, race, and education. Single men aren't losing out because of discrimination, however; married men consistently earn more money because they typically work harder and better.

Studies have also shown that married couples experience less economic stress. Married men tend to make more money than single men, and married couples tend

> Mortality charts underline marriage's profound longevity benefit. The risk of dying drops substantially for men right after they get married.

to make more money than single people. They also are more conservative when it comes to spending it. Single people are much more likely to spend their money engaging in unhealthy and risky behavior than those who have the responsibility of a family.

Mortality charts underline marriage's profound longevity benefit. The risk of dying drops substantially for men right after they get married. This is not the case for women (probably because they naturally tend to have less risky and more healthy lifestyles), but women eventually catch up. After several years of marriage, both husbands and wives reap an equal amount of health protection from taking their nuptial vows.

It doesn't take a rocket scientist to understand why. The reason for the dramatic initial boost to men's health after marriage is the positive influence of a good woman. Single men are extraordinarily vulnerable to a wide range of health and lifestyle problems. They drink more and deal more drugs, and they are more likely to commit, and be victims of, crimes. Single men are also involved in more accidents of every variety. No wonder single men rank lower in well-being and happiness than married men. Statistics indicate that unattached men kill themselves three times more often than married men.

Death of a Spouse

Sometimes we only realize how precious something is when we lose it. The stress of losing a spouse to death is second only to the stress caused by the death of a child. A spouse's death is so stressful, in fact, that it puts one at significantly increased risk for major health problems.

Men have an especially difficult time surviving a spouse's death. Researchers at the Johns Hopkins University School of Hygiene and Public Health found that men have higher death and illness rates after they are widowed, even after statistical adjustments for socioeconomic level, unhealthy behaviors such as cigarette smoking, length of marriage, and frequency of church attendance. Interestingly, the study found no significant differences in mortality rates between widowed and married females after adjustment for the same factors.

Research confirms that men are less likely to survive widowerhood because most do not have strong social support networks to rely on in times of need. They just don't have the same types of intimate relationships women do—not even with their own children. Many men do not make it a priority to develop deep friendship and support groups throughout their lives, relying instead on their wives to make social arrangements. Then, suddenly, those same men lose their social link to the outside world and find that they have no one to turn to for social support.

Widows, on the other hand, can usually call on a large safety net, woven from the close friendships and relationships they have maintained throughout their lives. Research shows that women of all ages tend to have more close and nurturing relationships than do men. It is that same social support network that they can call upon if their husband dies.

While marriage is good for your health, that doesn't mean you should run out and get remarried right after the death of your spouse. A marriage license isn't necessarily going to add years to your life. Married people still get sick, and they still die.

Divorce and Health

Those who are blessed with a solid marriage benefit from a positive self-image that comes from being "one-half of a couple." That deepest of human relationships can mean less stress in life and ultimately better health. Of course, that's not true for every couple. Married people who are independent of each other

> **What happens when the ties that bind begin to untangle and the marriage fails? What the research tells us is that when the marriage ends, so do the health benefits.**

or who have severe problems in their relationship do not benefit from that couple identity. And, without that sense of being well connected, such individuals are more likely to suffer health problems.

What happens when the ties that bind begin to untangle and the marriage fails? What the research tells us is that when the marriage ends, so do the health benefits. As soon as the divorce decree is signed, death rates of divorced men and women revert to the higher levels of their single friends. Divorced men are twice as likely to die prematurely from high blood pressure as married men. They are also twice as likely to die from heart disease, four times as likely to die prematurely from throat cancer, and seven times as likely to die prematurely from pneumonia. Moreover, scientists have known for 60 years that divorced men are at a tremendous risk for suicide.

In fact, so great are the negative health effects of divorce, scientists tell us, that being divorced and a non-smoker is only slightly less dangerous than being married and smoking more than a pack of cigarettes a day.

Friendship and Healing

Several years ago, twin sisters Brielle and Kyrie Jackson were born prematurely in Worchester, Massachusetts. At 2 pounds, 3 ounces, Kyrie was gaining weight and doing well. But the parents' joy turned to concern—followed by alarm—when it became apparent that their other tiny daughter was not thriving. Despite the best efforts of the doctors at the high-tech postnatal intensive care unit, Brielle had gained little weight, and her heart and respiration rates were declining. The hospital staff gently tried to prepare the shaken parents for the inevitable.

Then one of the babies' nurses remembered hearing about a double-bedding technique that was used for multiples in parts of Europe. Even though it was against standard procedures, with the parents' permission the nurse put the two siblings together. Not long afterward the excited nurse called for the staff to see something truly amazing. As the surprised nurses and doctors watched, Kyrie put a tiny comforting arm around her sister. What was even more astonishing was the change wrought by the comforting, loving touch of her sister. Little Brielle's condition began to improve immediately, and she made a full recovery.

If the encouraging embrace of a loved one can make a tiny newborn thrive, think of what it can do for us! As we have already indicated, the quality of our relationships and the depth of our social support also have an impact on our health. Practically any caring relationship—whether it's with a good friend and confidant or a co-worker—can make us healthier.

Making time for the people we care about will not only make us feel good, it can help us live longer, too. Remember, the immune system doesn't discriminate between a kiss from a spouse and a hug from a friend. It's the emotions we experience when we reach out to

> Love and intimacy are at the root of what makes us sick and what makes us well. I am not aware of any other factor in medicine—not diet, not smoking, not exercise—that has a greater impact.
>
> §
>
> —DR. DEAN ORNISH, *LOVE & SURVIVAL: THE SCIENTIFIC BASIS FOR THE HEALING POWER OF INTIMACY*

others—and when they reach out to us—that are so beneficial to our health. Constant, caring relationships take work, but in the long run, they're worth it.

We've already seen that women tend to live longer than men because women are better at making—and keeping—strong emotional ties outside of marriage. In a study of more than 300 people, Rubin discovered that very few of the men she interviewed could name a best friend. Those who did usually named a woman.

It's usually women who make lunch dates with girlfriends, write letters, make social plans, reply to invitations, and spend hours chatting on the phone. Intimacy is the hallmark of women's friendships. Very few men have these types of intimate relationships—they do things, they don't share things.

The tragedy in this difference is that the ability to reach out has a dramatic effect on how long we live and how healthy we are. Since the 1970s, study after study has shown that friendship and social support are crucial to our health and that, without such attachments, we're just not going to be as healthy as we should be.

Researchers in one study of nearly 7,000 residents of Alameda County, California, found that they could predict who would die within the next nine years simply by counting how many social ties the participants had. Based on this study and others like it, the California Department of Health launched a public service program pleading with residents to make a friend.

Friends can be good medicine indeed. Good social relationships can protect us from potentially fatal diseases ranging from tuberculosis to lung cancer to heart disease. One recent study found that people with lots of good friends had significantly less blockage of their coronary arteries than did those individuals who reported having very little social support in their lives.

In the story of little Brielle Jackson, we have seen the inexplicable yet very real power of emotional connection expressed through touch. If you still doubt the power of touch, consider this: In one study, when nurses held the hands of female surgical patients while their vital signs were taken, those patients left the hospital sooner and recovered faster at home than did women who had no similar physical contact with hospital workers.

PARISH NURSES

Long before researchers discovered the health benefits of caring friendship, the parish nurse movement was practicing the art of compassion. These registered nurses, who are deeply spiritual, offer their clients a combination of skilled medical care and prayer. They provide emotional support as well as practical help to people who often feel hopeless.

The significance of parish nurses in the lives of their clients cannot be overestimated. They are a combination of social worker, minister, nurse, patient advocate, friend, advisor, and guardian angel.

Those who have benefitted from the assistance of parish nurses can't praise them enough, saying that their help feels nothing short of miraculous. Some credit parish nurses with saving their lives, while others credit them with saving their spirits.

People caring for one another—that's what family is supposed to be about. Unfortunately, fractured families as well as an increasingly impersonal health care system leave many people without loving support. This may explain the explosive growth of the parish nurse movement, a centuries-old idea that gained new momentum with the publishing in 1985 of *The Parish Nurse* by Granger Westburg, a doctor and former hospital chaplain.

Today there are more than 6,000 parish nurse programs in the United States and abroad. Parish nurses work to improve their patients' physical, emotional, and spiritual health. About half of them are volunteers.

Janice Ruch, a parish nurse in the Advocate Health Care system in Chicago, explains the vital service the nurses provide: "Because of changes in recent years, many people are restricted from accessing services portioned out through managed care," Ruch says. "We used to work under a plan of care from the physician where the nurse would go in to dress a wound, and after 20 or 30 minutes, she had better be out of there and on to the next patient. But with parish nursing, we can take the time we need with each individual. Often, the best thing to give is a shoulder to cry on because grief and anxiety reduce the body's ability to heal physically."

Parish nurses are providing caring friendship to those they minister to. Their tremendous popularity underlines the powerful urge in the human heart to belong, as well as our deep need for social support. Modern society places supreme faith in medical technology to cure disease. But individuals need more than sterile, impersonal hospitals and efficient doctors who arrive at a diagnosis in a few minutes without developing a personal relationship with their patients.

IS IT IN THE GENES?

Some scientists suspect that the impulse to connect with others may be encoded in our genes. A person who is cut off from others is likely to suffer both physically and psychologically. Many of the strongest emotions that people experience are linked to feeling a sense of belonging and social support. We want to form new social bonds—by joining a new club, making a new friend, having a new child—and we are usually very reluctant to break these bonds. How many of us continue to send holiday cards once a year to individuals we never see or even call on the phone? How many people seem reluctant to break off a bad relationship, even one that causes physical or emotional pain?

Our need to belong is deeply rooted. Parish nurses and others who meet this need are helping patients become happier and more content. Like eating and sleeping, perhaps the urge to reach out to others is so strong because our very lives depend upon it. Without these relationships, our health is very likely to fail.

PETS KEEP YOU HEALTHY

The movie *The Horse Whisperer* told the true story of an intuitive rancher who cures physical and emotional injuries in people by helping to create an emotional bond between them and horses.

But Barbara Tomlinson, of Yuma, Arizona, didn't need to see the movie to believe in the curative powers of animals. She learned about that when her 12-year-old son began having emotional difficulties. In her search for help, she followed a most unusual path that led to using horses to alleviate her son's problems. Because of her experiences, Tomlinson has started a therapeutic riding program called Saddles of Joy that introduces children to what she calls "one of God's most beautiful creations, the horse."

More than 100 children have experienced emotional healing by bonding with a horse through Tomlinson's

program. "There's definitely a spirit in each horse that the children can sense; adults sense it, too, but it is more acute in children," Tomlinson says. "The horses can sense the need in the child and the child can feel the response. It's an unconditional response, an unconditional love that the horse gives the child."

Millions of pet owners would agree it's not so far-fetched to believe that one of the most important roles of horses and other domesticated animals is to provide loyal companionship as well as what Tomlinson calls "unconditional acceptance" of humans.

And, oh, how we all need unconditional acceptance! We've seen how marriage and friends can provide that. But not everyone is happily married. Others are divorced or widowed. Still others have never been married at all. Many people have lost touch with friends or are retired and have moved to a different part of the country, leaving friends behind. Whatever the reason, such individuals are often very much alone. But this doesn't mean they are destined to live a bleak existence fraught with poor health. It means they need to actively seek out a little companionship. The solution to loneliness may just be right around the corner—at the nearest humane society or animal shelter.

What Pets Provide

In recent years, we have become increasingly aware of the role of animals in combating the loneliness of spirit that affects so many people, especially the elderly. Animals are indispensable companions for many lonely people, essential therapeutic tools for people with a variety of psychological and emotional problems, and vital helpers to those who are physically handicapped.

> The feelings of intimacy we experience with our pets can increase our resistance to disease in the same way that human companionship seems to boost health.

Aaron Katcher, M.D., an associate professor of psychiatry at the University of Pennsylvania, found that the feelings we experience when caring for another living creature can actually boost our health. Katcher believes the companionship of animals may actually reduce the frequency of serious disease, as well as prolong life.

How do animals improve our health? According to Katcher, the feelings of intimacy we experience with our pets can increase our resistance to disease in the same way that human companionship seems to boost health.

The mere presence of an animal—even without direct contact—can lower blood pressure rates.

Children almost invariably respond positively to a friendly animal. In one study, children brought into an experimental setting had lower blood pressure when a dog was present with the experimenter, compared to when the experimenter was there alone. Blood pressure was lower in the presence of the dog whether the children were sitting quietly or engaged in the mildly stressful task of reading aloud.

The unconditional love given by a cat or dog can do wonders for mental health, too. After all, humans are fundamentally social beings. We need to reach out to others, and if there isn't another human around, a pet will do just as nicely.

Companion animal programs are popping up at nursing homes and various medical institutions around the country. These programs utilize the ability of animals to connect with humans. Animals are particularly useful in helping wheelchair-bound people interact with those around them. We all know how people with noticeable physical handicaps tend to be avoided or ignored by others—even by friends and family. Studies show that adding a companion animal to the picture increases quality and quantity of attention directed toward the disabled person.

Talk With the Animals

Can we learn how to communicate from watching how we talk to our pets? Curiously, when people speak to each other, their blood pressure levels almost always increase. But when people speak to their pets, their blood pressure levels remain the same or, in some cases, decrease.

In talking to an animal, people use a different pattern of speech than they do with other humans. They tend to speak more slowly and more softly, with a higher pitch, and in shorter sentences. Research has shown that this style of speech is associated with lower blood pressure.

People often stroke animals when they speak to them. Touching can be an effective method of reducing stress. Studies have shown that, in patients recovering from heart attacks, the simple act of touching the patient when taking his pulse can alter the heart rate and lower the likelihood of abnormal heart rhythms.

Many people consider their cats and dogs part of the family. Pets are often included in family photographs, they sleep on the bed or in the bedroom, and they provide constant companionship throughout the day. Some pets are talked to like people, and in a significant number of instances, pets act as silent confidants.

Especially during adolescence or during later life—when people become isolated by separation from or the deaths of spouses, relatives, and friends—animals may be intimate companions.

Pets and Longevity

Doctors at Johns Hopkins Medical Center in Baltimore found that patients recovering from severe illnesses who have pets live longer than those who don't. The numbers speak for themselves. One study showed that 50 out of 53 former patients who had pets were alive a year after their first heart attack; only 17 of the 39 patients who didn't have pets survived the year.

Losing a Pet

Those who have never lost a faithful pet of many years may not understand that the owner goes through a grieving process, especially if they depended on the pet for friendship and solace. The loss of a loved animal can hurt one's physical health and mental state.

Unfortunately there are few support mechanisms for those who have lost a pet, and there is a general lack of

acknowledgment among friends and family of the seriousness of such a loss. Indeed, individuals who lose their pets may conceal their grief for fear of ridicule or appearing weak.

Having to give up a pet can be as painful as having to bury one. Many elderly people lose their pets, not because of the death of the animal, but because they are forced out of their residences and into retirement or nursing homes, where pets are not accepted. Losing a pet in that way can be a severe source of stress that leads to depression or physical illness, says Katcher. Losing the pet's comfort and companionship only compounds the other losses—of independence, of familiarity of place, of worldly possessions—that the elderly pet owner is experiencing at the same time. No wonder depression and illness often follow.

THERAPY AND HEALING

Some people not only have lost their family and friends, but they don't even have a friendly pooch to fetch their slippers. Having absolutely no one to turn to breeds feelings of isolation, loneliness, and depression. For these individuals, psychotherapy may be beneficial. No matter what type of therapy is involved, studies have found that the bond that forms between a patient and a counselor can improve emotional and mental states.

Some may balk at seeing a therapist. It may be an irrational fear of being perceived as weak, or perhaps it doesn't seem right to have to pay someone to show interest and compassion. But we hire experts to help us with all kinds of things: We go to a dentist to fix our teeth and to a doctor to heal our body. Why shouldn't we make use of the services of those trained to help people facing emotional difficulties?

Psychotherapy helps boost healing, psychologists suspect, by fostering hope. Depression, hopelessness, and stress are all related to higher death rates in patients with coronary artery disease. Studies have shown that when patients with heart disease are given psychotherapy in addition to other treatments, they live longer and healthier lives.

Therapy not only nurtures hope, it can also improve your attitude. Studies have shown that people with positive attitudes (those who feel they have some control over both the present and the future) almost always heal more quickly than people who feel badly about themselves or their circumstances.

> Studies have shown that people with positive attitudes almost always heal more quickly than people who feel badly about themselves or their circumstances.

Researchers at Massachusetts General Hospital had psychiatrists spend time with patients who were recovering from heart attacks to see if there would be any positive benefits from their visits. Not surprisingly, patients who received consultation said they felt better and were less anxious and depressed. They were also more likely to survive their heart attacks. Similarly, psychologists at UCLA found that, even when differences in medication were taken into account, cancer patients who received supportive and educational home visits had significantly longer survival rates.

Another UCLA study assigned patients with malignant melanoma (a deadly form of skin cancer) to a series of weekly support groups designed to help them cope with the disease. The psychiatrists discovered that those who received therapy and support had better coping strategies and were less depressed than the group that

didn't participate in the therapeutic sessions. The UCLA team also found significant differences in immune system response between the two groups. When they looked at natural killer T cells (the type of white blood cells that kill invading cancer cells), the individuals who had participated in group therapy had more killer-cell activity.

The study indicated that the immune systems of the cancer patients had been strengthened by the group therapy. Even more encouraging, more than six years later, the patients who had participated in group therapy enjoyed substantially longer periods of remission, and fewer of those individuals ultimately died from the skin cancer.

The research shows that therapy can be an effective means for promoting physical as well as mental health. Experts believe the reason for this is that many diseases are "disorders of arousal." The hormones in the brain that are released by constant high levels of stress can lead to high blood pressure, migraines, Raynaud disease, irritable bowel syndrome, even asthma. Psychotherapy is one more tool that patients can use to ease stress and help them take an active part in their own health care.

SELF-HELP GROUPS

Since we know that having someone lend a sympathetic ear to your problems can make you healthier, it shouldn't be surprising that an entire group of interested listeners—the kind you find in a self-help group—can also boost your health.

That is, in fact, precisely what scientists have discovered. In a study of breast cancer patients in California, David Spiegel, M.D., randomly assigned 86 patients to attend either a weekly support group or only routine cancer care. After five years Spiegel was astonished to discover that, on average, patients who had been in the support group lived twice as long as the women who didn't attend the support group. This result held true regardless of how advanced their cancer was when they first joined the group.

In addition, there was a direct relationship between how long the women survived and the amount of time they spent in the support group. Those who

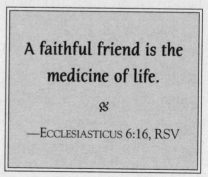

A faithful friend is the medicine of life.

❧

—Ecclesiasticus 6:16, RSV

never went to a session lived an average of 26 months. By comparison, those who went to between one and ten sessions survived 36.5 months, while those who went to more than 10 sessions survived 41.5 months.

One reason that support groups have an effect on longevity is that they are a safe place for people to express the pessimistic and depressing emotions that they may not feel comfortable expressing elsewhere. People participating in support groups can also share coping strategies and compare their experiences with others. It's a powerful way for people to mobilize their resources and face their diseases with courage. Self-help groups can help you rise above feelings of isolation or hopelessness, learn how to deal with various treatments and their side effects, and get the latest information on dealing with health care providers and insurance companies.

What should you look for in a self-help group? There are a number of things to consider. First, find a group of people who are in the same boat as you, facing problems similar to your own. Second, look for qualified leadership. Try to find a group that's led by a well-trained professional, whether that's a nurse, doctor, social worker, or psychologist.

Also, don't feel bad about not returning for a second visit if you don't feel the group is right for you. Take your time looking around, and don't settle for anything less than a group that you feel comfortable with—one that has a supportive atmosphere. You should feel comforted and respected. You might be upset at times, but you should feel that at least you have gotten a new perspective on your problem and a feeling of support and sense of confidence in your ability to handle a situation.

If a support group makes you feel judged for the problem you are facing or offers false promises and facile solutions, you're better off looking elsewhere. There is more than one perspective on every situation, and the group should listen to and respect different points of view. Finally, be wary of any group that asks you to kick in large amounts of money. Most self-help groups are free or have only nominal fees to cover expenses.

COMMUNITY HEALTH

Demographers in the 1950s and 1960s found a remarkable anomaly in the mortality rate of the town of Roseto, Pennsylvania. Despite the abundant presence of risk factors such as smoking, high fat intake, obesity, and a sedentary lifestyle, researchers found a remarkably low incidence of deaths from heart attack in the close knit Italian-American community. In 1965, the death rate from heart attacks in Roseto was half that of people in the neighboring community of Bangor.

Until then the townspeople of Roseto still embraced old-world values such as close family and community ties, a secure and respected place for elders, and a low level of social competitiveness.

However, things were slowly changing. As Roseto became more Americanized, it began to adopt the unhealthy social practices of its neighbors. Slowly but perceptibly, the traditional strong family and community ties in Roseto began to loosen. And as they did, the death rate from heart attacks began to climb.

By 1975, the death rates from heart attacks in this now thoroughly Americanized and modern town had reached the same level as that of Bangor and closely resembled that in the United States at large.

We've seen how healthy primary family relationships as well as supportive friends and family are important for good health. But there is another, wider influence on health: Your identity as part of a neighborhood or a town is also essential to well-being.

Studies conducted over the past two decades have suggested that the social support you find in your community can be vital to your body and your mind, protecting against everything from the common cold to depression. A sense of belonging can help ease the pain of grief, boost the immune system, and inhibit the development of serious disease.

> The social support you find in your community can be vital to your body and your mind, protecting against everything from the common cold to depression.

A century ago the average extended American family included relatives from several generations, the majority of whom grew up together in the same community.

There's been a sea change in American society when it comes to where we live our lives. Instead of putting down roots that last for generations, the average family stays in a neighborhood only several years before moving on. All too often people do not live in a locale long enough to get to know their neighbors, and they often don't bother to make the effort because it would only make the inevitable break more painful.

This dissolution of communities began with the upward mobility of the late 1940s and early 1950s. Americans began moving from place to place, accepting corporate transfers or higher-paying jobs, all in the quest for greater financial wealth and security. It became acceptable—and expected—for people to move away from their families and their roots in order to move up. The bonds holding families—and communities— together gradually weakened.

Today, one-fourth of all Americans live alone in separate households. Many live their lives behind closed doors and have few social bonds. There are fewer homes with children, who easily and naturally establish connec- tions with other children and families on the block.

Experts, however, believe that the trend toward isolation may be slowing down. Ironically, at a time when many of us feel that people and communities in our society are drifting farther apart, increasing numbers of Americans are rediscovering the importance of com- munity.

An example of changing attitudes towards com- munity is "co-housing," a Scandinavian concept that is

somewhere between an apartment complex and a commune. Co-housing is a way for individuals to fulfill their need and desire for community. The co-housing concept combines private living units with shared community facilities, usually with plenty of open green spaces in between. The majority of co-housing developments in this country, many of which include gardens, day care, volleyball courts, and a communal dining hall, are currently found in Washington and California. Co-housing is one way of reaching out and reconnecting the bonds between individuals and their community.

We've looked at the importance of social relationships, starting with the most fundamental—that of marriage and family—and expanding to include other care providers and ultimately the community in which we reside. Community life is more than an American way of life. It is one of the keys to good health.

Sometimes it's easy to forget about the resources we have around us. When you're feeling stressed, stop and think about who is out there for you. How big your social network is may well be less important than how you feel about the people you can call on for support. It's the depth of our relationships—not how full our dance card is—that counts when it comes to our health.

CHAPTER 7
When God Is Silent

& & &

"Why me, God?" Most of us have asked
this at one time or another. It's a completely
normal response when we or those we love are
stricken with life-threatening illness. There are
no easy answers to such heartfelt questions.
But we can be assured that our prayers are
not wasted even if they are not answered in
the way that we would wish. And though our
physical ailments are not always cured,
it is possible to find healing on deeper
and more fulfilling levels.

WHEN PRAYER DOESN'T WORK

When we—or those we care about—are not healed, it is perfectly normal to ask, "Where are you, God?" At one time or another, most people of faith have asked, "Why wasn't my prayer answered?" Throughout this book we've demonstrated that prayer can indeed work. But what about when it doesn't? Some say we must simply accept this as a mystery of faith. Yet it is human nature to want answers.

Unanswered prayer is a spiritual and theological problem, not a scientific one. And it is a problem not just because we don't get what we ask for, but also because the Scriptures—on which many people base their faith— do promise answers to prayer. In the book of Isaiah, for example, the righteous king of Israel, Hezekiah, prayed for healing from a terminal disease and was granted an additional 15 years of life (Isaiah 38:1–5).

For Christians, the promises of answered prayer recorded in the New Testament are unequivocal. Jesus promises his disciples, "So I tell you, whatever you ask for in prayer, believe that you have received it, and it will be yours" (Mark 11:24).

Perhaps prayer requires strong confidence that God will answer in order for it to be effective. Research has shown us that belief increases the effectiveness of any treatment. There is no reason why prayer should be any different.

But that would make the result dependent upon us "working up" a strong faith, when Jesus commanded us to have the faith of a little child. The fact is that there are times when healing prayer is offered in faith and healing does not come.

THE STRENGTH OF ACCEPTANCE

While suffering people always and understandably want an immediate end to their suffering, people of faith accept—sometimes wholeheartedly, sometimes with anguish—that God may have his reasons for allowing their suffering to continue. History is replete with examples of men and women who have endured great suffering without allowing their affliction to dampen their faith. As a result, they became extraordinarily strong and loving human beings who inspire the rest of humanity.

Great religious figures whose faith and devotion cannot be questioned have had their prayers go unanswered—or they weren't answered in the way they hoped. One of the towering figures of the New

Testament, the Apostle Paul, faced this very dilemma. Paul says, "a thorn was given me in the flesh, a messenger of Satan to torment me, to keep me from being too elated" (2 Corinthians 12:7). Most biblical scholars believe that this "thorn" was a physical malady. Although Paul implored the Lord for healing on three occasions, his prayers were not successful.

But there was a purpose for that "thorn" and for the many ways in which Paul suffered physically during his sojourns. The purpose was to help transform him into a great saint. God told Paul, "My grace is sufficient for you, for power is made perfect in weakness" (2 Corinthians 12:9). Paul understood God's message, declaring, "So, I will boast all the more gladly of my weaknesses, so that the power of Christ may dwell in me" (2 Corinthians 12:9). Though certainly painful to endure, Paul's physical suffering gave him a spiritual strength that he otherwise would not have had.

Just as affliction brought about change in Paul's life, so, too, may God choose to use illness to accomplish needed change in our own lives. We may not see or appreciate the final goal now, but we may be surprised to find we feel as Paul says he did: "Therefore I am content with weaknesses, insults, hardships, persecutions, and calamities for the sake of Christ; for whenever I am weak, then I am strong" (2 Corinthians 12:10).

MAKE NO JUDGMENTS

Paul's example also teaches us not to reproach others who pray for healing seemingly without effect. "Under no circumstances are we to tell those receiving prayer that it is their fault: that they lack the faith, or that there must be some sin in them that is hindering the prayer, or any such thing," writes Richard Foster in *Prayer: Finding the Heart's True Home*. "This will only redouble the burden they must carry. . . ." It is not for us to assign blame as to why someone's prayers were not answered.

Carter Morris, whose daughter Heyward is healthy because of a miraculous answer to prayer, is especially sensitive to those whose prayers have not been answered. In *Expect a Miracle*, author Dan Wakefield quotes her: "You hear the word miracle a lot now. I don't use it lightly. So many people don't get one," she says. "When Heyward was still in a coma and we didn't know if she'd ever recover, people came and told us their miracles of a child recovering, and I felt like throwing something.

> Our way of seeing these things is there is healing that happens even when there is not a cure. Bodies can be cured—or not, but at the same time there's a healing of a mind and of a spirit.
>
> ❧
>
> —REV. JAYNE YONKMAN, SPIRITUAL CARE MINISTER OF THE WEGE INSTITUTE FOR MIND, BODY, AND SPIRIT, GRAND RAPIDS, MICHIGAN

"We don't flaunt our miracle," Carter continues. "What do you say to those people who don't have one, whose children will be in a hospital the rest of their life? We visit people now in rehab who may be there for years or permanently. It's not fair."

FINDING THE MIRACLE

We believe—or desperately want to believe—that the stories of divine healing are true. But it hasn't happened for us. Could God have a different kind of healing in mind for us?

After the death of his son, Rabbi Harold Kushner wrote the book *When Bad Things Happen to Good People*. "Sometimes, we don't notice the miracle we actually get," said Rabbi Kushner. "We may ask God to take the tumor away, but the actual miracle may be that we get the resources to live with that tumor."

The resources Rabbi Kushner is talking about include the peace of mind to face difficult and painful surgery and treatment. Rev. Diane Morgan, director of pastoral services at William Beaumont Hospital in Royal Oak, Michigan, has seen the positive effects of prayer. "We are very careful not to push prayer on anyone," she says, "but patients are usually very open to prayer because something is wrong or suspected to be wrong. The result [from prayer] you can see almost immediately is the patient relaxes, and with relaxation can come lessened pain, a better outlook."

The healing we experience may take place on other levels than the physical, such as the restoration of broken relationships. Rev. Morgan says, "I don't believe in a capricious God who heals some people and not others. I don't think prayer is ever wasted even if prayer is not answered in the way we think it should be—everyone dies. But even if there is not physical healing, there is often healing in relationships, in family dynamics, in the person's attitude."

Dr. Jerome Groopman, chief of the division of experimental medicine at Boston's Beth Israel Hospital, offers a Jewish perspective on the art of healing. According to Groopman, the Hebrew Bible and the Talmud contain much wisdom regarding spiritual healing. Referring to the ancient Jewish "Misheberakh" prayer, Groopman says, "It asks God to heal the soul first and then the body. Why is physical healing secondary when petitioning God? I think it's because asking God for spiritual insight focuses you. Maybe we have to understand that the first priority is the healing of the soul. There will come a time when the healing of the body is impossible, so it's almost illusory to make it our first request."

The healing of the spirit, of emotions and relationships, then, is as great a miracle as any physical cure.

Just ask Brad Szczecinski. When his kidneys failed, he tried alternative medicine and attended the church he'd found just before he became ill. It was his way of trying to stay in control.

A few months later, though, only kidney dialysis was keeping Brad alive. Fearful, he began looking for something that would sustain his spirit. His pastor recom-

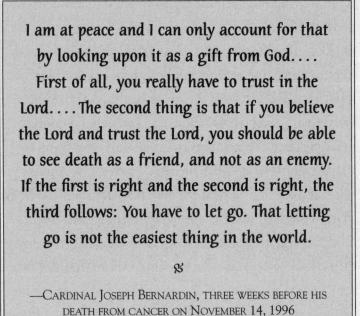

I am at peace and I can only account for that by looking upon it as a gift from God.... First of all, you really have to trust in the Lord.... The second thing is that if you believe the Lord and trust the Lord, you should be able to see death as a friend, and not as an enemy. If the first is right and the second is right, the third follows: You have to let go. That letting go is not the easiest thing in the world.

&

—CARDINAL JOSEPH BERNARDIN, THREE WEEKS BEFORE HIS
DEATH FROM CANCER ON NOVEMBER 14, 1996

mended that he attend a prayer meeting, which was led by Joe Barrett.

Two years before, Joe had found a new relationship with Christ, and he felt a special empathy for Brad, who seemed to be seeking the peace and sense of purpose that Joe himself had so recently found. Joe asked Brad to pray with him after the meeting, and that night Brad went home and accepted Christ.

Brad's health continued to deteriorate, however, and he was soon placed on the transplant list. After knowing Brad just two weeks, Joe offered to donate his kidney. Of the 21 people who volunteered, only Joe was both healthy enough and a match, even though he wasn't a relative. "It occurred to me that God has infinite ways of solving problems. And with his help, I have the power to be one of them," says Joe in explaining his generosity.

The operation was a success. Joe gave Brad a new chance at life. And with that chance, Joe has gone on to help others, taking every opportunity to share the good news of God's love.

ULTIMATE HEALING

Those who do not attain complete physical healing can experience valuable emotional and spiritual growth.

We have seen how the Apostle Paul struggled with unanswered prayer for a physical malady. His perspective can grant us comfort and strength in our darkest hours: "So we do not lose heart. Even though our outer nature is wasting away, our inner nature is being renewed day by day. For this slight momentary affliction is preparing us for an eternal weight of glory beyond all measure" (2 Corinthians 4:16-17).

If there was anyone who had a right to complain and be mired in discouragement, it would have been Paul. Yet despite the suffering he himself endured, Paul encourages us not to lose heart. The reason: All this is preparing us for "an eternal weight of glory." That is why, as Groopman notes, the first priority in the Hebrew Talmud is the healing of the soul. With a healthy spiritual outlook we will have the resources to maintain a positive outlook in the face of illness and disease.

IN THE END, THERE'S HOPE

As they fought desperately against the Nazi occupiers who were sending their compatriots to the death camps, Jewish partisans in Vilna, Poland, kept faith with the motto, "Never say you are walking on the last road."

Groopman, whose Polish grandmother lost her extended family in the Holocaust, prominently displays the saying in both Yiddish and English in his office. It can encourage each of us to hope and pray for divine intervention when—for each of us will likely have the opportunity—we find ourselves facing serious illness.

We have heard the testimonies of remarkable healings from cancer and "incurable" diseases. Others are learning, with God's help, to live—even prosper—amidst

Prayer of an Unknown Confederate Soldier

❦ ❦ ❦

I asked God for strength that I might achieve;
I was made weak that I might learn to obey.
I asked for health that I might do great things;
I was given infirmity, that I might do better things.
I asked for riches that I might be happy;
I was given poverty that I might be wise.
I asked for power that I might have the praise
   of men;
I was given weakness that I might feel the need
   of God.
I asked for all things that I might enjoy life;
I was given life that I might enjoy all things.
I got nothing that I had asked for,
but everything that I had hoped for.
Almost despite myself my unspoken prayers were
   answered;
I am, among all men, most richly blessed.

the uncertainty of chronic illness. And still others have fought the good fight and graduated to glory, having been strengthened to face life's greatest challenge.

We do not know where our own personal road will lead us. There will surely be mountaintop experiences as well as valleys of despair. Life is not fair. But it takes faith in God to believe that whatever happens is okay, because he has permitted it for a reason. It has wisely been said that while God does not always show up and perform a miracle, God always shows up.

That can give us hope in divine assistance in our hour of need. In the poem "Footprints in the Sand" (see page 75), God tells the young man that when there was only one set of footprints, it was then that he was carrying him. And so he will carry us all.